Neven Cooks

Neven Maguire

D1396656

POOLBEG

Published 2002
Poolbeg Press Ltd.
123 Grange Hill, Baldoyle,
Dublin 13, Ireland
Email: poolbeg@poolbeg.com

3 5 7 9 10 8 6 4 2

A catalogue record for this book is available from the British Library.

ISBN 1-84223-129-4

Photography by Kieran Harnett
Designed by Steven Hope
Typeset by Patricia Hope in Trebuchet 9/11

Printed by Betaprint
Unit 2A, Malahide Road Industrial Pk,
Dublin 17

www.poolbeg.com

Biography

Neven Maguire has been cooking alongside his mother since he was 12 in their award-winning restaurant in Blacklion, Co Cavan. Although Neven is still in his 20's he already has 15 years of cooking experience behind him and a string of awards. In 1996 he was 'Eurotoque Young Chef of the Year', in 1999 and 2000 he was 'Bushmills Chef of the Year' and in 2001 Neven represented Ireland in the prestigious 'Bocuse d'Or World Cuisine Competition' in France. Neven was a well-kept secret known only to foodies until three years ago when he took up residency in the *Open House* studio as Chef. Now his name is a byword for elegant, classic cooking without any fuss and he has viewers from Gweedore to Glandore rustling up risottos and searing swordfish.

This is Neven's first book, and he wants to teach everybody some simple starters, dinners, and some of the desserts for which he became famous while still a teenager. Neven's roaring trade in Sunday lunches illustrates the huge tradition that Sunday lunch still is in Ireland. He wants to help novices learn how to roast that lamb or cook that bird the right way, the first time! Neven also takes on Christmas, and shares with us the Yuletide recipes that have passed through his family for generations.

Whether you are cooking for yourself, for elaborate dinner parties or for fussy children, this book has you covered for most eventualities. Neven's measurements are precise and offer imperial and metric scales (though he does recommend that you make the recipe in *either* metric quantities *or* imperial). Each recipe is accompanied by a colour photograph of the finished dish and detailed instructions are provided to help you replicate it.

Neven includes plenty of helpful tips with each recipe and as he says himself: "If I can source these ingredients from a small village in Co Cavan, they should be easily accessible in any area!" So get stuck in, and enjoy cooking the way Neven cooks.

Acknowledgements

I am delighted to acknowledge the love and support that I have always received from my parents, Joe and Vera. They encouraged me from a very early age to develop my interest in cooking and were by my side, helping me whenever they could. Best supporting act is, as ever, my large family of eight brothers and sisters, all of whom have been there for me when things got hectic and especially while writing this book. Special thanks to my Auntie Maureen whose Christmas recipes I reproduce, and my dear Granny, whose influence is everywhere in the book. Also to the people of Blacklion, the village in Cavan where I live – a better community you couldn't wish for! And thanks to all the customers who come to MacNean Bistro, without whom food means nothing – they bring the entertainment and the atmosphere.

Over the years in the restaurant I have been lucky to meet some wonderful people who have taken the time to encourage and advise me as I try to improve my cooking skills. They are all the chefs who have inspired me, some of whom I count as friends, especially Neil McFadden and the wonderful Lea Linster. I would also like to thank John and Sally McKenna, Georgina Campbell, Gillian Bolger, Tom Doorley, Katrina McGirr, Olan McGowan and Marian Campbell for their support. Thanks also to Michael Doherty of *TV Now* who first published my recipes when he launched his magazine.

I always maintain that my cooking owes a lot to the quality of the ingredients I use. I'm lucky to be near so many excellent suppliers especially Mark Murphy and Paul Boee.

RTE's *Open House* has had a huge effect on my life. It has taken me out of the confines of my kitchen and the small community of Blacklion and into people's homes. I still can't believe it when I'm out shopping how many people come up to me to discuss food. I love it, and will never tire of talking food matters with them. Mary Kennedy and Marty Whelan have always been wonderful to me on the show. The producer, Larry Masterson and staff are like family to me.

It took a long time to compile this book from scratch, but I wasn't alone. Along the way, there was a dedicated team making it happen. Starting with the kitchen staff in MacNean: special thanks to Robert, Carmel and William for their tireless efforts with the food. In Tyrone Productions thanks are due to Patricia Carroll and Michael Scott who managed to get it published and so helped me achieve one of my dearest ambitions. We spent some hectic days cooking all the recipes for the photo shoot and we managed to keep our sense of humour throughout. This was thanks to Regina Looby and Kieran Harnett the photographer, whose enthusiasm, dedication and artistry has produced such wonderful photographs. Finally, with love and thanks to Amelda, for her constant help and support throughout.

For Dad
Who always encouraged me to write a book
and was constantly in my thoughts as I did

Contents

Smoked Salmon Rolls with Cream Cheese and Red Onion

Serves 4

It seems every house or office party I go to has smoked salmon of some sort on offer. We can't get enough of it! So that's why I'm including a starter with smoked salmon. These are really easy to make and can be made ahead of time, which is always handy. You can have them as a starter or make lots of them as snacks for a party.

Ingredients
1 red onion, finely diced
12 oz / 350 g pre-sliced smoked salmon
3 oz / 75 g cream cheese
2 tablespoons crème fraîche
1 rounded tablespoon finely chopped chives

4 large slices of wheaten bread
1 lemon ($^1/_2$ zest only, $^1/_2$ sliced for garnish)
8 whole chives with flowers if in season
Seasoning

Method   In a small bowl combine the finely diced red onion with $^1/_4$ pint / 150 ml of boiling water and drain off immediately. This softens the raw flavour of the onion. Mix together the cream cheese, crème fraîche, chopped chives and red onion. Season to taste.

On a sheet of clingfilm, place 3 slices of smoked salmon together, overlapping slightly to make 1 large slice. Spread the cream-cheese mixture on the salmon. Roll into a neat sausage shape. Repeat this process with remaining slices and keep chilled in the fridge until ready to serve. Using a small scone-cutter, cut 4 rounds out of each slice of wheaten bread.

To Serve   Slice each chilled smoked salmon roll into 4 small rolls and lay each roll sideways on a bread round. Place 4 rounds per person on a plate, garnish with some lemon zest and serve with lemon slices (and chives with flowers if in season).

Tip   When buying smoked salmon, make sure you know what you're really getting. 'Irish smoked salmon' may only be smoked in Ireland, but 'smoked Irish salmon' is definitely Irish and in my opinion it's the best.

Creamy Garlic Mushroom Vol-au-vents

Serves 6

These little vol-au-vent cases are so easy to get and I always keep some in the freezer on stand-by. This sauce can be rustled up in minutes for a fantastic supper dish.

Ingredients

1 tablespoon olive oil
1 onion, diced
3 garlic cloves, crushed
1 lb / 450 g button mushrooms, quartered
1/2 pint / 275 ml cream
1/2 pint / 275 ml milk

2 rounded teaspoons cornflour
2 tablespoons water
6 large vol-au-vent cases, frozen
Seasoning

Method Preheat the oven as per vol-au-vents packet instructions.

Heat oil in a pot on a medium heat and fry the onion and garlic for about 2-3 minutes, until soft. Add the mushrooms and mix well. Leave to cook for about 6-8 minutes, until the mushrooms have cooked through. Next add the milk and the cream and bring to the boil. Mix the water with the cornflour, and add this to the sauce to thicken it. Bring it back to the boil. Reduce the heat and simmer for about 5 minutes, stirring occasionally, to let the flavours mingle. Season to taste.

Cook the vol-au-vents from frozen as per packet instructions.

To Serve Place each vol-au-vent on a plate, spoon the mixture inside and let some overflow. Put the lid on the case and serve with green salad.

Tip This sauce is great with pasta, or if you don't have the vol-au-vents you can just serve it on toast.

Warm Salad with Bellingham Blue Cheese

Serves 4

When I first started cooking, I thought it was a contradiction to have a warm salad – the very word salad implied cold lettuce, tomatoes and cucumber. But now, as we all know, a salad is as much about textures as the green stuff! This one is guaranteed to wake up your taste buds and you'll love the blue cheese, which is made by a friend of mine in Louth.

Ingredients
1 tablespoon oil
4 slices streaky bacon, cut into strips or lardons
4 slices of thick white bread, cubed (for croûtons)
8 oz / 225 g mixed organic salad leaves
2 oz / 50 g walnuts, chopped and toasted
2 oz / 50 g cherry tomatoes, quartered
2 oz / 50 g Bellingham blue cheese,
or any blue cheese

Dressing
2 tablespoons balsamic vinegar
4 tablespoons olive oil
1 teaspoon Golden Syrup
1 teaspoon wholegrain mustard
Pinch of brown sugar
Seasoning

Method First make the salad dressing by putting the vinegar, oil, Golden Syrup, mustard, sugar and some seasoning into a container with a lid. Shake vigorously until thick and smooth and keep in the fridge.

Heat the oil in a frying-pan and fry the bacon until crispy. Remove and keep warm. Then put the bread-cubes in the same pan and fry until golden brown and crunchy. Keep warm until ready to serve.

To Serve Prepare four individual portions of the salad leaves on plates. Crumble the cheese on top and sprinkle the bacon, walnuts, croûtons and cherry tomatoes over the plates. Drizzle the dressing over the salad.

● Tip We're so lucky to have Eden Plants just 10 minutes away from us here in Blacklion and we always have a great selection of unusual fresh lettuces available. However, Curly Endive, Lollo Rosso and Romaine are all easy to get and would be nice in this salad.

Chicken Liver Pâté with Onion Jam

Serves 6

I know how easy it is to buy pâté these days, but I love to make my own occasionally. This recipe can be prepared ahead and will keep for 3-4 days in the fridge. I love the contrast between the onion jam and the pâté.

Ingredients
14 oz / 400 g fresh chicken livers
$^1/_2$ pint / 275 ml milk
3 shallots, chopped
1 tablespoon port
4 oz / 110 g butter
4 eggs
1 garlic clove, crushed
1 tablespoon cream
1 level teaspoon chopped thyme
4 oz / 110 g unsalted butter, melted

Onion Jam
2 red onions, peeled and finely sliced
1 oz / 25 g butter
2 oz / 50 g brown sugar
3 fl oz / 75 ml red wine
$1^1/_2$ fl oz / 40 ml red wine vinegar
1 tablespoon water
Seasoning

Method To make the pâté, soak the livers in milk overnight and next day remove them from the milk and dry thoroughly with kitchen paper. In a hot frying-pan sweat the shallots, garlic and thyme in 1 oz / 25 g of butter for 2-3 minutes. Add the port and cook for another minute.

Preheat the oven to 180°C / Gas 4.

Purée the livers in a food processor for about 3 minutes. Then add the shallot, garlic and thyme, and blend for 30 seconds. Next add the eggs, cream and the remaining butter. Blend everything together and season well. Pass the mixture through a sieve and pour into a 1 lb / 450g bread tin lined with clingfilm (or you could use a Pyrex dish). Cover this with tinfoil and place in a roasting-tray half-filled with hot water (this is a bain-marie). Place in the oven for about 1 hour or until set. Leave to cool and then put in the fridge for 1-2 hours to chill. Lastly cover the pâté with the melted unsalted butter to preserve it.

For the onion jam, melt the butter in a pot and add the onions, wine vinegar, red wine and brown sugar. Cook for 5 minutes, then add the water and cook for a further 25-30 minutes. The onions should make a soft, sticky sweet and sour jam. Season to taste.

To Serve Scoop out a spoonful of the pâté and serve with the onion jam, toast triangles and salad leaves.

Tip If you're hungry and need a quick snack, forget the fancy stuff. Make some fresh white toast and spread the pâté on the hot bread. It's absolutely delicious.

Crispy Cheese with Sweet and Sour Sauce

Serves 2

Fried or grilled cheese is a very popular dish. Brie is good for frying as is goat's cheese if you like a stronger flavour. This sweet and sour sauce cuts through the richness of the cheese and the cranberries give a real bite. Serve with salad.

Ingredients
8 oz / 225 g cheese e.g. Brie, Camembert or Cáis Bán
$1/2$ teaspoon medium curry powder
$1/2$ teaspoon chilli powder
$1/2$ teaspoon sesame seeds
4 oz / 110 g breadcrumbs
1 rounded tablespoon plain flour
1 egg, beaten in a large bowl with some milk
Frying-oil at 160°C / 320°F.

Sauce
$1/2$ tablespoon olive oil
4 oz / 110 g mixed peppers, diced
1 rounded tablespoon diced onions
2 rounded tablespoons brown sugar
$1/2$ tablespoon dark soy sauce
$1/4$ pint / 150 ml vegetable stock
1 tablespoon wine vinegar
$1/2$ tablespoon tomato purée
1 tablespoon tomato ketchup
1 teaspoon cornflour mixed with 2 teaspoons of water
1 tablespoon shop-bought cranberry sauce
Seasoning

Method First make the sauce. Heat the olive oil in a pot and sweat the peppers and onion in it for about 1 minute. Then add the rest of the ingredients. Simmer for a few minutes until it has reduced a little. Check the seasoning. You can change the flavour of the sauce according to taste. To make it sweeter add some sugar and for a sharper flavour add some more vinegar. Simmer for another 3-5 minutes and keep warm until ready to serve.

Mix the curry powder, chilli powder, sesame seeds and breadcrumbs together and set aside in a wide bowl. Season the flour and set aside on a plate. Then cut the cheese into slices and dip first in the flour, then in the beaten-egg mix and lastly coat in the spicy breadcrumbs. Make sure it is well covered. Deep-fry until golden brown.

To Serve Drizzle the sweet and sour sauce around the deep-fried cheese and serve with a green salad.

●Tip This sauce can be kept in the fridge and is an excellent accompaniment to duck, turkey and cold meats such as pork. Make some extra to keep.

Warm Potato and Herb Pancakes with Crème Fraîche

Serves 4

My grandmother, Susan Maguire, still makes boxty for my family every Hallowe'en and Easter. I look forward to those meals as much as to my Christmas dinner. This is a modern version of boxty, which still uses a potato base but with more exotic toppings. Mind you, I have to say, I still prefer my Granny's plain old boxty.

Ingredients
Base
5 oz / 150 g plain flour
2 eggs
$^{1}/_{2}$ pint / 275 ml milk
3 oz / 75 g cooked potato
1 rounded tablespoon chopped parsley, chives and scallions
2 tablespoons frying-oil
Seasoning

Topping
2 oz / 50 g butter
4 oz / 110 g sliced mixed mushrooms
e.g. chestnut, shitake and button
2 baby leeks, washed and sliced
6 scallions, chopped
1 tablespoon basil pesto
2 tablespoons crème fraîche

Method Preheat oven to 180˚C / Gas 4.

Sieve the flour and a pinch of salt into a bowl and make a well in the centre. Break the eggs into the well and gradually pour in the milk, stirring continuously. Add the cooked potato and herbs and check the seasoning. Mix well to form a smooth batter similar in consistency to lightly whipped cream.

To make the topping, heat the butter in a hot frying-pan, add the mushrooms, leeks and scallions. Cook for 5 minutes on a low heat and season to taste.

To make each pancake, heat some frying-oil in a hot oven-proof frying-pan and drain off the excess. Pour a quarter of the potato pancake batter onto the frying-pan and cook over a medium heat for about 1 minute. Then put the frying-pan in the oven for about 6-8 minutes until the pancake has risen and set. Repeat process 3 times to make the rest of the pancakes.

To Serve Place each pancake on a plate and spread some mushroom mixture on top. Spoon a dollop of crème fraîche over it and drizzle with some pesto.

● Tip Taking the idea of the pancake, you can top it with other ingredients. The classic is bacon and cabbage, but some prefer seafood in a white sauce. You can come up with your own favourite combinations.

Creamy Prawn and Leek Tart

Serves 8

This is a great lunch or supper-time dish with a very creamy texture. I'd recommend that you use good-size prawns in it to really kick in the seafood taste.

Ingredients

Pastry
8 oz / 225 g plain flour (plus some extra to roll pastry)
1 rounded teaspoon caster sugar
4 oz / 110 g unsalted butter (plus extra to grease tin)
2 teaspoons cream
2 eggs
1 lemon, sliced, for garnish

Filling
1 oz / 25 g butter
4 oz / 110 g thinly sliced leeks
4 oz / 110 g cooked peeled prawns
1 teaspoon chopped herbs (dill or parsley)
3 eggs
1 teaspoon sweet chilli sauce
$1/4$ pint / 150 ml milk
8 fl oz / 225 ml cream
Seasoning

Method Preheat the oven to 180°C / Gas 4 and grease an 8-inch / 20 cm flan ring.

To make the pastry, mix the flour and sugar in a bowl. Rub in the butter until the mixture resembles crumbs. In a separate bowl, whisk the eggs and cream. Add this to the pastry, and mix together using your hands if necessary. Wrap in clingfilm and leave to chill in the fridge for at least 1 hour.

Next roll the pastry on a floured counter and line the tin with the pastry. Place in the fridge to rest for 30 minutes. Then cover with lightly oiled tinfoil and fill with baking beans. Bake blind in the oven for about 10 minutes or until golden brown. Take the tart out of the oven, remove the baking beans and the tinfoil.

Reduce oven temperature to 160°C / Gas 3.

To make the filling, sweat the leeks in butter in a frying-pan on a medium heat for about 4-5 minutes, add the prawns and herbs and heat through. Mix the eggs, chilli sauce, milk and cream in a large bowl. Stir the prawn-and-leek mix into the bowl and mix well. Season to taste. Pour the filling into the pastry and bake in the oven for about 40 minutes or until just set. Leave to cool for 10 minutes.

To Serve Serve a slice, with some lemon garnish and a nice green salad.

● Tip You could keep this vegetarian: leave out the prawns and you have a simple quiche.

Bruschetta with Wild Mushrooms and Asparagus

Serves 4

This dish uses the classic Italian bruschetta as its base but adds a different slant to the usual tomato topping. It could also serve as a light supper or snack and is especially tasty for vegetarians. If you prepare the sauces and bread in advance, you could make mini-bruschettas on rounds of country bread or small slices of baguette, and you have a perfect canapé or party food.

Ingredients
1 small onion, chopped
4 cloves garlic, peeled
1 lb / 450 g asparagus spears
1 lb / 450 g button mushrooms, diced
3 oz / 75 g wild mushrooms e.g. ceps or porcini, diced
4 slices country bread or baguette
3 fl oz / 75 ml olive oil

2 oz / 50 g Parmesan shavings (or grated)
Seasoning

Pesto
1 large bunch of basil leaves
2 cloves garlic, peeled
1 rounded tablespoon pine kernels
6 fl oz / 175 ml olive oil

Method First make the pesto: place the basil, garlic, pine kernels and olive oil in a blender for about 2 minutes. Season and set aside.

Next heat a teaspoon of the olive oil in a hot frying-pan, add the onion and 3 cloves of crushed garlic and sauté for 2 minutes. Add all the mushrooms and simmer on a low heat for 10 minutes. Season and keep warm.

Now prepare the asparagus by breaking off the tough parts at the bottom and peeling the stalks. Cook in boiling salted water for 4-6 minutes depending on size, drain and keep warm.

Lastly toast both sides of the bread under the grill. Now rub one side of the bread with a clove of garlic and drizzle the remaining olive oil on top.

To Serve Spread the mushroom mixture on top of each slice of toasted bread. Lay the asparagus spears on top and drizzle with the pesto. Garnish with sautéed mushrooms and Parmesan shavings.

● Tip Nowadays we can get exotic mushrooms just about everywhere. So check out some of the more exciting ones, like chanterelles, oysters and shitakes. They're delicious.

Hallowe'en Pumpkin Soup with Smoked Bacon

Serves 6

It's hard to believe it, but up until recently you'd have had a difficult task finding a pumpkin in any shop in Ireland. Nowadays the whole country seems to be scooping out pumpkins and making Jack-o'-lanterns for Hallowe'en. Not being a wasteful lot, we have started collecting new recipes so that we could cook something with all that wonderful orange flesh. This one's for a tasty soup, just the thing if you've been out 'trick or treating'!

Ingredients

1 oz / 25 g butter
1 onion, diced
4 oz / 110 g raw smoked bacon, diced
2 lb / 900 g pumpkin flesh, peeled,
de-seeded and cubed
1 tablespoon tomato purée
2 pints / 1.2 litres chicken stock

3 fl oz / 75 ml cream
1 tablespoon whipped cream
2 oz / 50 g cooked smoked bacon,
chopped for garnish
Seasoning

Method   Melt the butter in a large heavy-bottomed pot. Add the onion, raw smoked bacon and pumpkin flesh. Sweat for about 6-8 minutes to release the flavours. Add tomato purée and stir for 2 minutes. Then pour in the stock and stir in the cream. Cook on a low heat for 20-25 minutes. Liquidise with a hand-blender and season to taste.

To Serve   Pour soup into bowls, place a dollop of whipped cream in the centre and sprinkle the cooked bacon pieces on top. Serve with warm bread.

● Tip Pumpkin seeds are lovely sprinkled on salads. Instead of discarding them, wash, dry and toast them in a moderate oven for about 10 minutes. They'll keep for weeks in an airtight container.

Chunky Summer Tomato and Basil Soup

Serves 4

I'm a big fan of eating soups throughout the year, as they are so easy to make and so satisfying to eat. But I'm always surprised that so few people think of making soup in the summertime. So to tempt you to eat more summer soups, here is one of my favourites. You need lots of fresh tomatoes, which are at their ripest, juiciest and cheapest in the summer. With all the flavours of the garlic and basil, you'll think you're in Tuscany.

Ingredients
1 tablespoon olive oil
1^1/$_2$ lb / 700 g fresh tomatoes
1 onion, peeled and chopped
2 garlic cloves, peeled and crushed
1 rounded tablespoon chopped basil
1 tablespoon tomato purée
1 bay leaf
1^1/$_2$ pints / 850 ml vegetable stock
1 tablespoon low-fat crème fraîche
Seasoning

Method Chop the tomatoes into chunks. Heat the oil in a large pot and add in the tomatoes, onions, garlic and basil. Let this mixture simmer for 2-3 minutes or until the vegetables are softening. Then add the tomato purée and stir in for about 2 minutes. Add the bay leaf and pour in the vegetable stock. Bring to the boil stirring constantly and leave to simmer for 15-20 minutes on a low heat. Season to taste.

To Serve Serve in a bowl with a small dollop of crème fraîche and some herb bread.

● Tip If you are making soups like this one for vegetarians, do remember to use vegetable stock. If it has chicken or beef stock, it isn't vegetarian.

Rossnowlagh Seafood Chowder

Serves 6

If you like fish, you'll love chowder - and if you like chowder, you'll love this recipe. It's easy to make and the ingredients are available everywhere nowadays. In fact, I noticed recently that some supermarkets even sell chowder mixes in their frozen-food section, complete with squid rings, shelled prawns and juicy mussels.

Ingredients

1 oz / 25 g butter
1 onion, diced
1 leek, diced
2 carrots, diced
2 large potatoes, diced
1 rounded tablespoon plain flour
$^1/_4$ pint / 150 ml white wine
2 pints / 1.2 litres fish stock
4 oz / 110 g salmon fillet, skinned and cubed

4 oz / 110 g smoked cod fillet, skinned and cubed
4 oz / 110 g whiting fillet, skinned and cubed
4 oz / 110 g mussels
4 oz / 110 g king prawns
$^1/_4$ pint / 150 ml cream
1 rounded teaspoon chopped parsley
1 rounded teaspoon chopped dill
Seasoning

Method Melt the butter in a large heavy-bottomed pot over a medium heat. Sweat the onion, leek, carrots and potatoes in the butter for about 5 minutes or until they are soft. Add the flour and cook on a low heat for 2 minutes, stirring constantly. Slowly stir in the white wine followed by the stock. Bring to the boil and simmer for 5 minutes. Add in all the prepared fish and let the soup simmer for another 10 minutes. Stir in the cream and season to taste. Finally, sprinkle in the chopped herbs.

To Serve Place in a warmed bowl and serve with some crispy bread, making sure that everyone gets some of the mussels and prawns.

●**Tip** When preparing this soup, be careful not to add the fish too early. You can make the basic soup well in advance, but once you add the fish it should be served immediately. Reheating the soup can cause the fish-chunks to break down and the soup loses its texture.

Hearty Winter Vegetable Soup with Barley

Serves 4

I created this recipe one day to use up some leftover vegetables. I gave some to my mother and I was delighted when she told me it tasted just like the soups she used to eat as a little girl– needless to say she loved it. It is true that this soup tastes kind of old-fashioned and really comforts on a cold wintry day. Take it from my mum!

Ingredients

2 oz / 50 g barley, washed
8 oz / 225 g carrots, diced
4 oz / 110 g onion, diced
4 oz / 110 g leeks, diced
4 oz / 110 g turnips, diced
4 oz / 110 g parsnips, diced
4 oz / 110 g celery, diced
2 oz / 50 g butter

2 oz / 50 g plain flour
4 pints / 2.2 litres hot chicken stock
1/2 pint / 275 ml milk or cream
1 scallion, chopped
1 oz / 25 g croûtons (toasted cubes of white bread)
Seasoning

Method Place the barley in a saucepan with 1/2 pint / 275 ml of cold water. Bring to the boil and simmer until cooked. Drain and set aside. Now heat the butter in a large heavy-bottomed pot, add all the diced vegetables and sweat for 5 minutes or until they are soft. Remove the pot from the heat and stir in the flour thoroughly. Put the pot back on a low heat and cook for 2-3 minutes. Then gradually add the hot stock, stirring constantly, and bring to the boil. Add the cream or milk, whichever you prefer, and season. Lastly, stir in the cooked barley.

To Serve Serve in a warmed bowl with croûtons, chopped scallions and crusty bread.

● Tip If you have any cold bacon leftovers in the fridge, chop them up and add them to this soup.

Classic Italian Lasagne

Serves 6-8

This dish needs no introduction as the Irish have taken to it as if it was our own. While it takes a long time to prepare, it is always worth the effort.

Ingredients
8 oz / 225 g lasagne sheets, pre-blanched in boiling water
1 tablespoon olive oil
1 onion, sliced
2 cloves garlic, crushed
8 oz / 225 g button mushrooms, sliced
2 lb / 900 g lean minced beef
1 carrot, peeled, trimmed and diced

2 tablespoons tomato purée
1 can chopped tomatoes
2 tablespoons soy sauce
1 tablespoon balsamic vinegar
1 level tablespoon sugar
1 rounded tablespoon chopped basil
4 oz / 110 g grated white Cheddar cheese
$^1/_2$ oz / 10 g butter (to butter dish)

Sauce
2 oz / 50 g margarine
2 oz / 50 g plain flour
1 pint / 570 ml milk, hot
1 pinch nutmeg, grated
Seasoning

Method Melt the margarine in a pot. Make a roux by adding in the flour and cooking for 3 minutes over a medium heat, stirring constantly. Gradually add in the milk, and stir until smooth. Simmer for 10 minutes. Add some grated nutmeg and season to taste. Set aside and keep warm until ready to assemble the lasagne.

To make the meat sauce, heat the oil in a large frying-pan, add the onions, garlic and mushrooms and cook for 5 minutes. Add in the mince and carrot and stir until lightly browned. Then stir in the tomato purée and cook for about 1 minute, followed by the chopped tomatoes. Stir well and add in the soy, vinegar, sugar and basil, then simmer for 15 minutes. Check seasoning and adjust to taste.

Preheat the oven to 160°C / Gas 3.

To assemble the lasagne: First butter an ovenproof dish and cover with a layer of the pasta sheets. Next place a layer of the meat filling on top and repeat this process twice until you have 3 layers in total. Cover with the white sauce and sprinkle with cheese. Cook in the oven for approximately 20-25 minutes.

To Serve Place the dish on the table and serve the family directly!

Tip This basic meat sauce can be used with spaghetti to make an authentic bolognese sauce. Just sprinkle grated Parmesan cheese over the dish before serving.

Best Ever Home-made Beefburger

Serves 4

All children love burgers, but what about the adults? It seems that we never grow out of our fascination for this meaty sandwich. Well, this is my Cavan contender for the Best Ever Burger and it caters specifically for the 'older children' out there. It's rather exotic and uses fresh pineapple and Gruyère cheese. Make sure you make one for yourself while you're at it

Ingredients

4 fl oz / 110 ml mayonnaise
1 teaspoon sweet chilli sauce
1 tablespoon olive oil
1 small onion, diced
2 cloves garlic, crushed
1 lb 5 oz / 600 g lean minced beef
1 rounded tablespoon chopped sage
2 eggs, beaten
4 rings fresh pineapple

8 thin slices Gruyère cheese
2 hamburger buns, halved
1 Spanish onion, sliced into thin rings
2 oz / 50 g plain flour, seasoned
2 oz / 50 g rocket leaves
2 vine-ripened tomatoes, sliced
Frying oil heated to 180˚C / 350˚F
Seasoning

Method First make the chilli mayonnaise by mixing mayonnaise and chilli sauce together. Keep in the fridge until ready to serve.

Now sweat the onion and garlic in half the olive oil for 2 minutes on a medium heat. Cool the mixture a little before putting it in a bowl with the mince, sage and eggs. Mix well and season. Shape into 4 large burgers. In a frying-pan, cook the burgers on a high heat in the remaining olive oil for about 6-7 minutes on each side or more if you prefer. You can also grill these or use the barbeque in the summer.

While the meat is cooking, grill the pineapple until hot and the juices are caramelising, then place 2 slices of Gruyère cheese on each pineapple ring and leave under the grill to melt. Dip the onion rings in the seasoned flour and deep-fry in the oil. Remove when golden and crispy and leave to drain on some kitchen paper. Toast the burger buns.

To serve On each toasted bun, place a small amount of rocket followed by 2-3 slices of tomato and a beefburger. Put a cheesy pineapple ring on the meat and top it all with some crispy onion rings. Drizzle the chilli mayonnaise over the open burger.

● Tip If you're making this for the children, use Easy Singles cheese instead of Gruyère, omit the pineapple and use plain mayonnaise. And, of course, you'll need a whole bun for each child.

Peppered Fillet of Beef with Green Peppercorn Sauce

Serves 4

Everyone loves a tasty sauce with their steak and this is a very simple sauce for you to try. I've included home-made chunky chips in the recipe, which is my favourite, but steak goes great with creamy mashed potatoes or a cheesy gratin. Whether you cook your steak on the stove-top or on the barbeque, make sure that you quickly seal the meat on a high heat to retain all the juices.

Ingredients
1 tablespoon olive oil
4 fillet steaks 6 oz / 175 g each
1 teaspoon butter
4 oz / 110 g spinach, washed
and stalks removed
2 large potatoes, peeled and
cut into thick chips

2 large Spanish onions, peeled
2 oz / 50 g plain flour
Salt and freshly-ground
black pepper
8 whole chives, for garnish
Frying oil heated to
180˚C / 350˚F

Sauce
1 oz / 25 g butter
1 shallot, chopped
5 oz / 150 g button mushrooms, sliced
1 rounded tablespoon whole green peppercorns
4 fl oz / 110 ml whiskey
1/4 pint / 150 ml beef stock
1/4 pint / 150 ml double cream

Method Preheat the oven to 180˚C / Gas 4.

First make the sauce. Melt the butter in a hot frying-pan, add the shallot and mushrooms and cook for 2 minutes. Add the green peppercorns and the whiskey. To remove some of the harsh alcoholic taste of the whiskey you can burn it off by putting a lighted match to the frying-pan. It will flame up for about 5-10 seconds and then subside. When the flame burns off, stir in the stock and slowly add the double cream. Reduce to a sauce consistency, which will coat the back of a spoon and season to taste. Set aside and keep warm until ready to serve.

Next prepare the vegetables. Melt the butter in a pot, add the spinach, and cook over a low heat until it wilts. Season and keep warm. For the chips, dip the potatoes quickly in the hot oil and drain on kitchen paper. Reheat the oil. To prepare the onions, cut them into very thin rings and sprinkle with salt. Leave to stand for 2-3 minutes and then toss in the flour. Shake off the excess flour and deep-fry until golden and crispy. Leave to drain on some kitchen paper and keep warm.

Now you're ready for the steaks. Grind plenty of coarse black pepper over them. Heat the olive oil in a large ovenproof frying-pan until it's smoking and put the steaks on it. Make sure you don't overcrowd the pan or the steaks will 'stew'. Cook each side of the meat for no more than 1 minute to seal in the juices.

Place the frying-pan in the oven for 3-10 minutes depending on how you want the steaks (3 minutes for rare, 7 for medium and 10 for well done). When cooked to your satisfaction, leave the meat to rest in a warm place and save any juices that run off the meat for your peppercorn sauce.

Now deep-fry the chips for a second time. This will make them very crispy and a nice golden colour. Remove and drain on kitchen paper.

To Serve Place spinach on the plate, put the steak on top, then spoon the sauce over it and top with the crispy onions. Place the chips at the side of the plate and garnish with some chives.

Venison Goulash with Creamy Mashed Potato

Serves 6

The number of calls I get on *Open House* asking me what to do with venison is amazing. Some people have received a gift of a venison haunch or others just see it on supermarket shelves and want to do something with it. So this is especially for those of you who haven't tried venison. It's a variation on a classic Hungarian stew, and looks very elegant if presented in the right way.

Ingredients

5 oz / 150 g butter
2 lb / 900 g venison haunch, cut into 1 inch cubes
1 lb / 450 g baby shallots, peeled and halved
2 oz / 50 g paprika
2 oz / 50 g plain flour
1 tablespoon tomato purée

3 pints / 1¾ litres beef stock
8 oz / 225 g carrots, peeled and cut into chunks
1 rounded tablespoon chopped parsley
1 lb / 450 g potatoes, peeled
¼ pint / 150 ml milk, heated
Seasoning

Method Preheat oven to 200°C/Gas 6.

Heat 3 oz / 75 g of the butter in a large heavy casserole pot. Season the venison, add to the pot and stir quickly. Add the shallots and cook for 2 minutes stirring constantly. Add the paprika and the flour, mix well and place the casserole pot in the oven for 5 minutes. When time is up, remove from oven and reduce the oven temperature to 180°C / Gas 4.

Put the casserole pot on a low heat and stir in the tomato purée. Then pour in enough beef stock to cover the meat. Bring to the boil and season. Cover with a lid and return to the oven for 1½ hours. Then remove from the oven, add the chopped carrots and continue cooking in the oven for another 30 minutes or until the meat and vegetables are tender.

Meanwhile boil the potatoes, drain and mash them. Add the rest of the butter and the warm milk. Season to taste.

To serve Place one portion of mashed potato in the centre of a bowl or plate. Arrange some meat, vegetables and sauce around it and sprinkle with a little chopped parsley.

● Tip To make this dish a 'one-pot' dinner, just chop the potatoes into chunks and add to the casserole with the carrots.

Sweet and Sour Pork with Rice Pilaff

Serves 4

Quite a few of my friends love sweet and sour pork and they eat it in restaurants regularly, but for some reason they never attempt to cook it themselves at home – they think it's too difficult. Well, not any more – here's a really easy sweet and sour sauce recipe.

Ingredients

2 pork fillets, trimmed and sliced
1 tablespoon sunflower oil
1oz / 25 g butter
1 red, 1 yellow and 1 green pepper, chopped into small cubes
1 onion, diced
1 clove garlic, crushed
1 rounded teaspoon grated root ginger

$^1/_4$ fresh pineapple, peeled and cubed
2 tablespoons white wine vinegar
2 oz / 50 g brown sugar
2 tablespoons tomato purée
2 tablespoons soy sauce
2 pints / 1.2 litres chicken stock
1 rounded teaspoon cornflour
Seasoning

Pilaff

2 oz / 50 g butter
1 oz / 25 g red onion, finely diced
4 oz / 110 g basmati rice
8 oz / 225 ml chicken stock
1 rounded tablespoon chopped parsley and coriander

Method Preheat the oven to 200°C / Gas 6.

Melt the butter in a hot pot. Toss in the peppers, onion, garlic and ginger and stir well. Next add the pineapple, vinegar, sugar, tomato purée, soy sauce and stock. Cook this mixture for about ten minutes and season to taste. Check for sweetness or sourness of the sauce. If it is too sharp then add some more sugar, and if it's too sweet add some vinegar. Lastly, mix the cornflour with 2 teaspoons of water until smooth. Add this to the sauce to thicken it slightly.

In a frying-pan, heat the sunflower oil and add the pork. Stir-fry for about 5 minutes until golden brown. Transfer the pork to the sweet and sour sauce and check the seasoning again. Leave to simmer on a low heat for 20-25 minutes.

For the rice: melt half the butter in a small casserole pot, add the onion and cook for 2-3 minutes until soft. Next toss in the rice and stir for 2 minutes. Pour the stock over the rice, season and cover with buttered greaseproof paper. Bring to the boil, then place pot in hot oven for approximately 15-20 minutes Remove from oven and stir in the rest of the butter and the chopped herbs. Keep warm until serving.

To Serve Arrange rice on the side of plate and spoon the sweet and sour pork beside it.

● Tip Pilaff rice is a great accompaniment for a special occasion, but of course you can also serve it with boiled or steamed rice. But do use basmati, as the delicate fragrance of the rice really complements the oriental flavours.

Glazed Pork Kebabs

Serves 4

A simple orange marmalade-based marinade gives this classic combination of pork and apricots a very special lift. Of course, when the fine weather arrives, you can cook these on the barbeque and serve with a salad.

Ingredients
1 lb 5 oz / 600 g boneless pork, trimmed of fat
12 apricots dried and ready to eat
2 small courgettes cut into 1-inch chunks
2 red onions, peeled and quartered
4 large skewers, wooden or metal

Marinade
4 oz / 110 g fine shred orange marmalade
2 tablespoons orange juice
2 tablespoons wholegrain mustard
$^1/_2$ teaspoon ground ginger
$^1/_2$ teaspoon dried thyme or oregano
Seasoning

Method Melt the marmalade in a pot over a gentle heat. Stir in the orange juice, mustard, ginger, thyme (or oregano) and seasoning. Set aside and leave to cool completely.

Next for the pork: cut the meat into $1^1/_2$-inch cubes. Place in a large bowl, pour the cold marinade over it and mix well together. Leave to marinate in the fridge for at least 2-3 hours. As with most marinades the longer you leave it the better the taste. If possible, refrigerate overnight.

To make the kebabs, thread the pork, apricots, courgettes and onions alternately onto four skewers. Place a griddle-pan or a large frying-pan on a medium heat and fry the kebabs for 20-25 minutes. Turn them regularly and brush with the leftover marinade. When the pork is cooked, remove kebabs from the pan and keep warm. Place the rest of the unused marinade in the frying-pan, heat and keep warm until ready to serve.

To Serve Place the kebabs on a large heated serving-plate and drizzle the hot marinade over them.

● Tip If using wooden skewers, it's best to soak them in water for about an hour before using them so they don't dry out too much or burn in the oven. The best skewers to use are bamboo and you can usually get them in specialist Asian shops and some supermarkets.

Rack of Sligo Lamb with Herb Crust

Serves 4

Lamb is a huge favourite in the Maguire household and it is rarely off our restaurant menu. They say you can taste the flavours of the countryside where a lamb is reared and certainly that is true of the wonderful lamb we get here in Cavan/Sligo, where the flavour of wild garlic sometimes permeates the meat. Irish lamb is at its best between March and September.

Ingredients

2 racks of lamb, trimmed
(your butcher will do this for you)
2 oz / 50 g breadcrumbs
Small bunch of basil, mint & parsley
1 teaspoon Dijon mustard
1 teaspoon olive oil
8 oz / 225 g fresh spinach,
stalks removed

1 oz / 25 g butter
8 fresh whole chives for garnish

Red Wine Sauce

1 tablespoon balsamic vinegar
$1/4$ pint / 150 ml red wine
1 rounded teaspoon brown sugar
$1/4$ pint / 150 ml beef stock
1 rounded tablespoon chopped thyme

Gratin

$1/2$ pint / 275 ml cream
$1/4$ pint / 150 ml milk
4 garlic cloves, crushed
Pinch nutmeg
1 lb / 450 g potatoes, peeled and
thinly sliced
2 oz / 50 g Cheddar cheese
Seasoning

Method Preheat oven 160°C / Gas 3.

First make the gratin. Heat the cream and milk in a pot. Add the garlic and nutmeg and season well. Arrange the potatoes neatly in an ovenproof dish, making sure the top layer looks really nice and pour the sauce over them. Cover the dish with greaseproof paper and tinfoil and place in the oven for 1 hour. Remove, sprinkle with the cheese and return to the oven for another 10 minutes or until the cheese is brown and bubbling on top. Remove and keep warm.

Now for the red wine sauce: Heat a small pot, and pour in the vinegar and red wine. Boil until reduced by half. Add the sugar, stock and thyme, and reduce to a sauce consistency, which should coat the back of a spoon. Pass the sauce through a sieve, season to taste and keep warm.

Meanwhile melt the butter in another small pot on a medium heat and cook the spinach until soft and wilted. Keep warm.

Increase the oven temperature to 180 C / Gas 4 and prepare the lamb. Blend the breadcrumbs with the fresh herbs in the food processor for 2-3 minutes. Brush lamb flesh with the mustard and then press the herb crumbs onto the mustard side of the lamb. Heat the olive oil in a frying-pan, put the lamb in and seal it on all sides for about 2 minutes. Place on a roasting dish. Put in the oven for 8-10 minutes if you like your lamb pink in the middle. If you want it well done, leave it in for 15-20 minutes.

To Serve Place some spinach on a plate and spoon some gratin beside it. Slice the lamb and place some on the spinach. Drizzle the sauce around it and garnish with 2 chives.

● Tip These racks can also be bought and shaped into a 'crown' for a really stunning visual effect on the table – guaranteed to make an impression.

Grilled Chicken Caesar Salad

Serves 4

So few people like anchovies in their Caesar salads that I've stopped putting them in mine. However, everybody seems to want chicken in it. I think people basically like the thick crunchy salad leaves and the creamy dressing of a Caesar salad - so for them, here it is, my way.

Ingredients
4 oz / 110 g day-old bread, cubed
1 head of Cos lettuce, washed
2 chicken breasts 8 oz / 225 g each
1 oz / 25 g Parmesan, grated
3 oz / 75 g cherry tomatoes, quartered

Dressing
1 free-range egg
1 clove garlic, crushed
2 teaspoons Dijon mustard
1 tablespoon extra-virgin olive oil
A few drops Tabasco sauce (optional)
$1/2$ teaspoon Worcestershire sauce
4 oz /110 g low-fat natural yoghurt
Seasoning

Method Preheat oven to 180°C / Gas 4.

Place the bread-cubes on a baking sheet and bake in the oven for 4-5 minutes until they are crispy, golden croûtons. Set aside and leave to cool.

Now make the dressing. Put the whole egg in a food processor along with the garlic, mustard, olive oil, Worcestershire sauce and yoghurt. Add the Tabasco if you are using it. Blend for 1-2 minutes in a food processor, season to taste and store in the fridge.

Next grill the chicken. Put the breasts on a baking tray and season with salt and pepper. Place the tray under a hot grill and cook for 8-10 minutes on each side. The chicken is cooked when the flesh is firm to the touch. Don't overcook or the chicken will dry out.

To Serve Place some lettuce leaves in a bowl and put some slices of grilled chicken on top. Toss in some Parmesan and cherry tomatoes and drizzle with lots of dressing. Repeat with a second layer and sprinkle some croûtons on top.

●Tip Best lettuces for this salad are Cos, Little Gem or Romaine. They are sturdy, crispy greens and have a great texture. If you're stuck, you could substitute Iceberg lettuce for the texture.

Supreme of Chicken with Lemon and Basil Risotto

Serves 4

Chicken is a hugely popular dish in Ireland and, for that reason, I have included plenty of chicken recipes in this book. This is one of my personal favourites. It marries fragrant oriental flavours with a touch of the Mediterranean.

Ingredients
4 Supremes of Chicken
(breast with bone attached)
1 oz / 25 g five-spice powder
2 oz / 50 g butter
1 clove of garlic, crushed
4 oz / 110 g onion, diced
8 oz / 225 g Arborio rice
(or any risotto rice)

1 pint / 570 ml chicken stock
1 rounded teaspoon lemon zest
1 rounded tablespoon chopped basil
2 oz / 50 g Parmesan, grated
1 tablespoon of port
1 tablespoon balsamic vinegar
Basil leaves for garnish
Seasoning

Method Sprinkle the five-spice powder over the chicken and season. Melt the butter in a large pot over a medium heat, add the garlic and onion and sauté for 2 minutes. Add the Arborio rice and stir well for 2 minutes, making sure to coat the rice grains well with the butter and onion mix. Gradually stir in the chicken stock and the lemon zest. Simmer for about 20 minutes, stirring occasionally throughout. When the rice is almost cooked (there will still be a small bite to it), add the basil and Parmesan, season well and keep warm.

For the sauce, simply reduce the port and vinegar in a small pot for 5 minutes or until the mixture becomes thick and syrupy. Keep warm until serving.

Finally place the chicken under a hot grill and cook for 8-10 minutes on each side. It will be firm to the touch when cooked.

To Serve Place some risotto in the centre of a warmed bowl or plate. Sit the Chicken Supreme on top and drizzle a little of the syrup around the rice. Garnish with some fresh basil.

● Tip Your butcher will prepare Supremes of Chicken for you, but if you can't get them, don't let it stop you making this dish – you can use regular breasts of chicken instead.

Summer Barbeque Chicken Drumsticks

Serves 4

This dish can be cooked in the oven at any time, but there's no doubt that the drumsticks taste fantastic when they've been cooked outdoors on a barbeque. So get some in next time you hear the temperatures are set to rise.

Ingredients
16 chicken drumsticks
2 tablespoons tomato ketchup
1 tablespoon soy sauce
2 tablespoons balsamic vinegar
2 oz / 50 g brown sugar
1 teaspoon wholegrain mustard

1 orange, rind and juice
1 tablespoon Golden Syrup
1 tablespoon tomato purée
1 tablespoon chopped parsley, for garnish
Seasoning

Method Mix all the ingredients, except the chicken and garnish, in a large bowl and season. Place the chicken drumsticks in the marinade making sure to coat them well. Cover and leave for at least 3 hours or, better still, overnight in the fridge.

Preheat oven to 190˚C / Gas 5.

You can cook these drumsticks in a preheated oven for approximately 25-30 minutes or cook them outdoors on the barbeque.

To Serve Pile them high on a big plate, garnish with some parsley and watch them disappear!

Tip Always take care when cooking chicken on the barbeque. It must be cooked right through and not just on the outside. Take extra care when handling raw chicken especially in the summer heat. Always wash your hands after working with it and clean down any surfaces or utensils used in the preparation of the meat.

Poached Breast of Chicken with Smoked Bacon Mousse

Serves 6

There's no doubt that this is a rather fancy dish. While it is well within most people's ability to cook, it is a little tricky and is not something you'd rustle up for a regular family meal. However, if it's a special occasion, then this is the dish to impress. It looks so delicate on the plate but really has a very strong taste and texture. Give it a go and see what you think.

Ingredients

5 chicken breasts
1 oz / 25 g butter
1 egg white
4 fl oz / 110 ml cream
2 slices smoked bacon, diced
1 tablespoon chopped mixed herbs: chives, parsley and basil

Dash balsamic vinegar
1 teaspoon tomato purée
$^{1}/_{4}$ pint / 150 ml beef stock
3 fl oz / 75 ml cream
3 oz / 75 g wild mushrooms, sliced: ceps, shitake or oyster

1 packet fresh tagliatelle pasta, cooked to packet instructions
Chervil for garnish
Seasoning

Method For the mousse stuffing, put 1 chicken breast in the food blender and mince thoroughly. Then add the egg white to the chicken, followed by the cream. Blend for 1-2 minutes. Season and then stir in the bacon and herbs.

To prepare the chicken, place the breast between sheets of clingfilm and flatten down with a rolling-pin or heavy object. When the breast is thin and flattened to twice the size, place a quarter of the mousse stuffing lengthways along it. Roll the meat over the stuffing to form a sausage shape. When rolled, wrap each breast tightly in some clingfilm to keep its shape. Twist the ends of the clingfilm, so that each looks like a Christmas cracker. Repeat process 3 times for each chicken breast. Keep in the fridge until ready to cook.

Now make the sauce. Place a pot on a medium heat, add in the vinegar and tomato purée, and reduce for about 2 minutes. Then pour in the beef stock, cream and finally the mushrooms. Stir well and reduce until the mixture has a sauce consistency and will coat the back of a spoon. Season to taste. Keep warm until serving.

Cook the tagliatelle according to packet instructions.

Meanwhile, poach the breasts of chicken (still wrapped in their clingfilm) in a pot of simmering water for 10-12 minutes, making sure that the water just covers the chicken. Then remove from the pot and peel off the clingfilm. Heat the butter in a large heavy-bottomed frying-pan and gently sauté the chicken. After about 3-4 minutes, remove from pan and keep warm.

To Serve Cutting at an angle, slice each chicken breast into 4 pieces, lay in a crescent shape on a plate and drizzle the mushroom sauce around it. Twist some freshly cooked tagliatelle in a spiral shape at the side. Garnish with chervil.

● Tip We always use free-range or organic chicken at the restaurant in Blacklion and I would really urge people to do the same. There is no doubt that the difference in flavour and texture is enormous. It is more expensive, I know, but personally, I'd rather eat less of the tasty organic chicken than more of the alternatives.

Cajun Chicken Supper

Serves 4-8

Because we love it so much, here's a great chicken dish. So simple, but it has fantastic Cajun flavours to heat it up – an ideal supper or lunch.

Ingredients
4 small French baguettes
4 chicken breasts, skinless
4 oz / 110 g Cheddar cheese, grated
3 tablespoons mayonnaise
2 rounded teaspoons Cajun spices
Mixed salad leaves for garnish
2 oz / 50 g sweet chilli sauce
Seasoning

Method Preheat the oven to 180˚C / Gas 4.

Sprinkle the chicken breasts with Cajun spices, season and place on a baking tray. Cook in the oven for about 15-20 minutes. The chicken should be springy to the touch when cooked.

Mix half the chilli sauce with the mayonnaise and season. Slice the baguettes in half and toast on one side. Now slice the cooked chicken breasts into thin slices.

Drizzle the mayonnaise over each slice of bread and place the sliced chicken on top. Sprinkle the Cheddar cheese over the chicken and drizzle some chilli sauce on top. Place under the grill and cook until golden brown on top.

To Serve Serve piping hot with some salad.

● Tip This is a great dish for a sudden influx of hungry people – so fast and easy to prepare. Everybody can help.

Duck Confit with Honey and Clove Sauce

Serves 4

Now this is a truly old-fashioned dish. Years ago the fat from the duck was used to preserve the duck before fridges came on the scene. Nowadays we don't need to do that, but cooking the duck in the fat still gives it such a wonderful flavour. Of course, if you cannot get any duck fat, you could substitute sunflower oil instead.

Ingredients
4 duck legs
1 clove garlic, chopped
6 whole star anise
3 oz / 75 g coarse sea salt
8-10 sprigs fresh thyme
1½ pints / 850 ml duck fat
(or sunflower oil)
1 orange, sliced

Vegetables
1 carrot, peeled and cut into small cubes
12 asparagus spears, peeled and trimmed
4 oz / 110 g broad beans, blanched
and skinned
2 oz / 50 g butter
Pinch of caster sugar
4 oz / 110 g spinach, washed,
with stalks removed

Honey and Clove Sauce
2 tablespoons clear honey
1 tablespoon soy sauce
1 tablespoon balsamic vinegar
1 rounded tablespoon brown sugar
1 tablespoon tomato ketchup
1 teaspoon whole cloves
4 fl oz / 110ml beef stock
Seasoning

Method First, sprinkle the garlic, star anise, sea salt and fresh thyme on the duck legs. Wrap them tightly in clingfilm and place in the fridge overnight to let the flavours infuse the duck meat. Next day, rinse the excess spices off the marinated legs, removing all the salt, and dry thoroughly with kitchen paper.

To cook the duck, heat the fat in a large pan and put the legs into the fat. Add the orange slices and simmer the legs very gently on a low heat until tender. This should take about 4-5 hours and you'll know the duck is cooked when the flesh is just coming away from the bone. Turn off the heat and leave to cool in the fat. When ready to serve, crisp the duck under a hot grill for 5-6 minutes or until crispy.

For the honey sauce, put the honey, soy, vinegar, sugar, ketchup, cloves and stock in a small pot, boil for approximately 5 minutes or until juices have thickened to a sauce consistency which coats the back of the spoon. Then season to taste. Keep warm.

To prepare the vegetables, place the carrots, asparagus, broad beans, and 2 tablespoons of water in a pot with a tight-fitting lid. Place on a medium heat for about 4-5 minutes or until just cooked. Strain and allow to cool slightly. Then heat the 2 oz / 50 g of butter in a frying-pan, add the sugar and the vegetables and toss. Give them a good stir and season to taste. Heat the spinach in another pot with just a tablespoon of water and cook on a low heat until wilted. Season well and keep warm.

To serve Arrange the reheated duck legs on top of some spinach. Place the sweetened vegetables beside it on the plate and drizzle the clove sauce around the duck.

⬤ Tip If you are watching your waistline, I should warn you off this particular dish as it is quite fatty – but so tasty! Maybe you might save it for a special occasion.

Breast of Duck with Mushroom and Wine Sauce

Serves 2

Duck is yet another meat that has become commonplace on our supermarket shelves. It gives the poultry-lover something a little different. People are always asking me on *Open House* for recipes for breast of duck and this is the one I always recommend.

Ingredients
2 duck breasts, Peking duck preferably
1 level tablespoon black peppercorns, roughly ground
2 oz / 50 g butter
4 cloves garlic, peeled
4 oz / 110 g fresh spinach, stalks removed
4 oz / 110 g button mushrooms
Seasoning

Sauce
1 tablespoon balsamic vinegar
1 tablespoon duck or beef stock
1 tablespoon red wine
Pinch brown sugar
1 level tablespoon chopped thyme

Method First put the spinach in a small pot with a tablespoon of water and cook on a low heat until wilted. Drain immediately and place on kitchen paper and set aside. In a hot frying-pan, fry the mushrooms in half the butter until just cooked, season and keep warm.

Grind the peppercorns onto the duck breasts and press down well. Season with salt. Then heat the rest of the butter in a frying-pan until it bubbles, place the duck breast skin-side down on the pan. Toss the whole garlic cloves into the frying-pan with the duck. Fry the meat for 5 minutes each side for rare meat, and 7 minutes for well done. Keep warm until serving.

Pour the balsamic vinegar into the empty duck frying-pan, bring to a boil and add the wine, sugar, thyme and stock. Reduce heat and simmer until it reaches a sauce consistency and will coat the back of a spoon. Season to taste.

To Serve Reheat the spinach and mushrooms and place on the plate. Cut each duck breast at an angle to give 3 pieces, and arrange on top of the vegetables. Drizzle the sauce over the duck.

● Tip Peking duck is one of the best varieties of duck to cook with. It is one of the smallest and has the most flavour. I always serve creamy mashed potato with this dish.

Grilled Salmon Cutlets with a Creamy Lemon Sauce

Serves 4

When I was young, the salmon we ate at home was always a cutlet on the bone, whereas these days I find that people want fillets of salmon. But for this recipe, I thought I'd use that old-fashioned cutlet and show how great it looks on a plate.

Ingredients
4 cutlets of scaled salmon, 7 oz / 200 g each
1 tablespoon olive oil
$1/2$ lemon, juiced
1 oz / 25 g butter
20 green asparagus spears
4 sprigs fresh dill for garnish

Lemon Sauce
1 shallot, finely chopped
$1/4$ pint / 150 ml white wine
$1/4$ pint / 150 ml cream
2 oz / 50 g butter, diced
1 lemon, juiced
1 tablespoon chopped chives
1 tablespoon diced tomatoes
Seasoning

Method First make the sauce by placing the shallot in a small pot, cover with the wine and cook over a medium heat for 2-3 minutes until the wine has evaporated. Whisk in the cream and reduce to a sauce consistency (this will take about 5 minutes). When ready, it will coat the back of a spoon. Next whisk in diced butter gradually. Season and stir in the lemon juice, chives and diced tomatoes. Set aside and keep warm.

Now peel and cook the asparagus in boiling salted water for 1 minute. Remove from pot and then refresh quickly in cold water to stop them cooking further.

To prepare the fish, generously coat the salmon with the olive oil, a squeeze of lemon juice and seasoning. Cook on a red-hot griddle-pan or under a hot grill. This should take only about 4-5 minutes on each side, as you don't want to dry out the fish. Reheat the asparagus with the butter in a hot frying-pan.

To serve Place the salmon cutlet at the side of the plate and carefully arrange the asparagus beside it. Drizzle with the creamy lemon sauce and garnish with dill.

Tip Griddle-pans are a fantastic way of cooking meat, fish and poultry. They allow you cook with less oil, are capable of very high temperatures and most of all they leave lovely caramelised ridge-marks on the skin.

Pan-fried Mackerel with Polenta and Tomato Stew

Serves 4

Nowadays you'll often hear people on radio and television talking about 'good fats' and 'bad fats', and they urge you to eat more oily fish for your intake of 'good fats'. Well, let me tell you that mackerel is one of the best examples of a good oily fish. As well as this important health factor, mackerel is also great value for money and has a lovely meaty texture.

Ingredients
4 mackerel fillets
1 oz / 25 g butter
Flat parsley for garnish

Tomato Stew
1 tablespoon olive oil
1 onion, sliced
1 clove garlic, crushed
4 tomatoes, cut into chunks

Dash red wine vinegar
1 rounded teaspoon sugar
1 teaspoon tomato purée

Polenta
8 oz / 225 g polenta flour
1$^{1}/_{2}$ pints / 850 ml vegetable stock
4 oz / 110 g butter
4 oz / 110 g Parmesan, grated
1 oz / 25 g melted butter

Pesto
2 bunches basil
3 oz / 75 g Parmesan
2 oz / 50 g pine nuts
2 cloves garlic
$^{1}/_{2}$ pint / 275 ml olive oil
Seasoning

Method First make the polenta. In a large pot, bring the vegetable stock to the boil and whisk in the polenta flour. Continue to stir until it starts to thicken (this will take only about 4-5 minutes). Then stir in the butter and Parmesan until melted through and the mixture comes away from the sides of the pot. Season and pour this wet mixture onto a greased Swiss-roll tin and spread evenly. Leave to cool for about 1 hour.

Make the pesto by putting the basil, Parmesan, pine nuts and garlic in a blender. Season and blend for 1-2 minutes. Add the olive oil and blend again, keep in a jar or a squeeze bottle in the fridge.

For the tomato stew, heat the tablespoon of olive oil in a small pot, add the onion and garlic and cook gently for 1-2 minutes. Add the tomatoes, vinegar, sugar and tomato purée. Stir well and season to taste. Let this stew cook slowly until the mixture dries out a little - about 5 minutes should do it.

When the polenta has set, cut it into rectangular shapes and brush with the melted butter. Fry the rectangles on a griddle-pan or place under the grill until browned and crispy on top. Set aside, and keep warm.

For the fish, score the flesh of the mackerel 3 times on each side. Heat the butter in a hot pan and place the fish skin-side down and cook for 5 minutes. Turn over and cook for a further 5 minutes.

To Serve Place polenta in the centre of the plate and spoon some tomato stew beside it. Place fish on the polenta and garnish with some flat parsley.

●Tip If you haven't tried polenta yet, take this opportunity to give it a go. Italians love it almost as much as pasta and it's a great substitute for our own favourite carbohydrate, the potato.

Elegant Fish and Chips

Serves 2

This is so simple. All you need is a really nice piece of fresh fish and the batter will enhance the texture and the flavour. It looks so good on the plate that I had to find a better name than Fish and Chips.

Ingredients

2 cod fillets 7 oz / 200 g each
2 oz / 50 g plain flour
1 egg beaten in a bowl
4 oz / 110 g breadcrumbs
Sunflower oil for deep-frying

4 large potatoes, peeled and cut into chips
1 lime, halved
Flat parsley for garnish
Seasoning

Method Heat the oil in a deep-fat fryer to 150° C / 300°F and cook the chips until soft. Remove from the oil and drain on some kitchen paper for 5 minutes while the oil reheats. Then put them back in the fryer and let them cook until they are very crisp and golden brown. Remove from the oil and season with salt immediately. Set aside and keep warm until ready to serve.

Raise the sunflower oil to 160°C / 320°F. Season the flour. Take the cod fillets and coat generously with the flour. Then dip into the beaten egg until well covered. Let the excess drip off. Finally dip the fillets into the breadcrumbs making sure they are completely coated. Deep-fry until crisp and golden.

To Serve Place fish on a plate, put half a lime beside it and build up a stack of chips behind the fish. Garnish with flat parsley.

Tip I always deep-fry chips twice. There is not enough heat in the oil to get them crispy unless you dip them in oil quickly to start them off – then let the oil re-heat and you're ready to crisp them up. Maris Pipers are the best potatoes for chips as they have less moisture content, but failing those I find Roosters work well.

Roast Monkfish on a Leek and Bacon Mash

Serves 4

Monkfish is a round, ugly fish that has become hugely popular in Ireland over the last five years. I find that people who normally won't eat fish enjoy this one. It has quite a chewy texture, quite like meat in some ways.

Ingredients
4 monkfish fillets, trimmed 6 oz / 175 g each
2 tablespoons olive oil
4 oz / 110 g streaky bacon, diced
3 oz / 75 g butter
3 oz / 75 g leeks, washed and sliced
4 oz / 110 g buttered mashed potatoes
Flat-leaf parsley for garnish

Sauce
$1/4$ pint / 150 ml red wine
$1/4$ pint / 150 ml beef stock
1 rounded teaspoon caster sugar
1 sprig thyme
1 teaspoon balsamic vinegar
1 teaspoon tomato purée
Seasoning

Method Preheat oven to 200°C / Gas 6.

Heat half the oil in a frying-pan, cook the bacon until just browned and remove to a dish. Now heat half the butter in the same frying-pan and sweat the leeks for 2 minutes or until just cooked and soft. In a pot, reheat the mashed potato and add the hot leeks and bacon to the mash. Check for seasoning, but remember that the bacon in the mash is already very salty. Keep warm until serving.

Now make the sauce. Heat the wine in a pot until it reduces by half. Next add the beef stock and reduce again by half. Add in the sugar, thyme, vinegar and tomato purée and stir for 2 minutes. Take off the heat and keep warm. Remove the sprig of thyme and season before serving.

To prepare the fish, heat the remaining butter and oil in an ovenproof frying-pan until foaming. Place the fish in the frying-pan and cook for 2 minutes on each side until golden brown. Season and place frying-pan in the oven for about 3-5 minutes.

To Serve Spoon some mash into the centre of a warmed plate, put the monkfish on top and drizzle the red-wine sauce around the mash. Garnish with some flat-leafed parsley.

● Tip We love our spuds in Ireland and for that reason I am always experimenting with them. I love this mash because it uses the traditional Irish ingredients of bacon and leeks. I discover all sorts of combinations to spice up my spuds, so don't be afraid to do the same.

King Scallops with Balsamic Lentils and Basil Purée

Serves 4

Scallops have such a beautiful natural sweetness and a wonderful light texture. I find these lentils really complement the scallops and make this a meal to remember. I'd recommend that you make this dish only when you can get the scallops fresh.

Ingredients
12 king scallops, shell and coral removed
1 tablespoon olive oil
4 oz / 110 g Puy lentils, soaked overnight
1 rounded tablespoon carrot, finely chopped
1 rounded tablespoon onion, finely chopped
$^1/_4$ pint / 150 ml beef or chicken stock
1 rounded teaspoon sugar
1 tablespoon balsamic vinegar
1 teaspoon tomato purée
Seasoning

Basil Purée
4 oz / 110 g basil leaves
4 fl oz / 110 ml olive oil

Crispy Carrots
2 carrots, peeled
1 rounded tablespoon plain flour
1 teaspoon salt
Frying oil pre-heated to 180˚C / 350˚F

Method Rinse the lentils in cold water and place in a saucepan, cover with water and bring to the boil. Add salt and simmer until the lentils are tender (about 15-20 minutes). Keep an eye on them though, as you may need to add more water. Drain the cooked lentils and return the saucepan to a low heat. Add the chopped carrot, onion and enough stock to cover the lentils and cook for about 10 minutes or until the lentils absorb all the stock. Next add the sugar, vinegar and tomato purée and stir well. Season to taste and keep warm.

For the basil purée, blanch the basil leaves in boiling water for 10 seconds and refresh in a bowl of iced water. Remove and pat the leaves dry and put in a blender. Season, add the olive oil and blend for 1-2 minutes.

Now prepare the crispy carrots, by slicing them into very thin 'julienne' strips. Lightly season with salt and dredge with flour, coating them lightly but completely. Deep-fry until light and golden. Drain on kitchen paper, season to taste and keep warm.

Finally, prepare the scallops. Cut each scallop in half horizontally to give you 2 smaller scallops. Heat the olive oil in a frying-pan until smoking and place the scallops in the pan. Cook for 20-30 seconds on each side until browned and caramelised. Be careful not to overcrowd the pan with the scallops as they will 'stew' and lose their crispness.

To serve Spoon the lentils onto the centre of the plate and place 6 half scallops in a circle on top. Drizzle the basil purée around the plate and garnish with the crispy carrot.

● Tip When making this dish, do use Puy lentils (or 'Lentils du Puy' as they are sometimes called). They are a special French variety with a delicate texture. It's quite easy to pick up tins of these lentils and they will work just as well as the dried ones – just bypass the 'boiling lentils' stage.

Gratin of Cod with Prawns and Gruyère Cheese

Serves 4

Cod and prawns are so popular that I've put them together to make this tasty and satisfying recipe. There's an overload of basil in this dish, but it sure gives a perfect contrast to the fish. This would be lovely with some baby boiled potatoes and a fresh green salad.

Ingredients
4 fillets of boned skinless cod 6 oz / 175 g each
6 oz / 175 g prawns, shelled and cleaned
4 oz / 110 g Gruyère cheese, grated
4 oz / 110 g sweet chilli sauce
1 rounded tablespoon chopped basil
4 oz / 110 g basil pesto

Wine Sauce
1 shallot, chopped
1 tablespoon oil
4 fl oz / 110 ml white wine
$1/4$ pint / 150 ml cream
$1/4$ pint / 150 ml fish stock
4 oz / 110 g basil pesto
Seasoning

Cabbage
$1/4$ head Savoy or York cabbage
2 oz / 50 g butter
2 tablespoons water

Method Preheat oven to 200°C / Gas 6.

First make the wine sauce. Heat the oil in a small pot on a medium heat, add the shallot and cook for 2 minutes, or until soft. Then add the wine and simmer until the mixture has reduced by half. Whisk in the cream and fish stock and reduce again to a sauce consistency that will coat the back of a spoon. Season and add the pesto. Blend the sauce with a hand-blender to lighten it. Set aside and keep warm until serving.

Next, chop the cabbage into large strips and wash under cold running water. Heat the butter in a large frying-pan over a moderate heat. Add the cabbage and water and fry for 3-4 minutes until soft and wilted. Season to taste and keep warm.

Now cook the fish. Place cod in an ovenproof dish. Spoon the prawns, pesto and sweet chilli sauce over the cod. Sprinkle the cheese and fresh basil over the top and cook in the oven for 8-10 minutes. When ready, the fish should flake when pressed with a knife.

To Serve Place the cabbage in the centre of a warmed plate, place the cod on the cabbage with a fish slice and drizzle the wine sauce around the fish.

●Tip Like most recipes using cod, you can replace it with other round white fish such as hake or haddock.

Tempura of Sole with Lemon Mayonnaise

Serves 6

This dish sounds very posh, but really it's just deep-fried battered fish. The batter I'm using here is quite a hot and spicy one, more suited to adults I think, than younger palates. You can substitute skate, plaice or sole for this recipe. You could also use the tempura batter to deep-fry vegetables such as broccoli florets, sweet potato slices and whole baby sweetcorn.

Ingredients
1$^1/_2$ lb / 700 g fresh sole, boneless fillets, trimmed
$^1/_4$ pint / 150 ml mayonnaise,
home-made or shop-bought
1 lemon, juiced
1 rounded teaspoon chopped chives
2 egg whites
2 tablespoons cream
Frying oil heated to 180°C / 350°F
Seasoning

Spice flour
6 oz / 175 g plain flour
Large pinch of white pepper
$^1/_2$ teaspoon salt
1 rounded tablespoon sesame seeds
1 rounded teaspoon chilli powder
1 rounded teaspoon medium curry powder

Method First make the lemon mayonnaise by mixing the plain mayonnaise with the lemon juice and chives. Check for seasoning and keep in the fridge until ready to serve.

Whisk the egg whites and cream together in a bowl and set aside. In a separate bowl make the spice flour by combining all the spice flour ingredients and mixing well.

Cut the sole into small slices and dip into the egg mixture, making sure it is well coated. Shake off the excess and dip the fish into the spice flour, coating it completely. Deep-fry for about 2 minutes or until golden and crispy. Take out and drain on some kitchen paper.

To Serve Place 3 pieces of the sole on a plate. Drizzle with some of the mayonnaise and serve with some dressed salad leaves.

Tip When deep-frying, I find the best oil to use is sunflower oil. It gets good and hot and doesn't burn. If you don't have a deep-fat fryer, use the heaviest pot you have e.g. cast iron or stainless steel. Always test before you fry – I use herbs to see how fast the oil reacts. Keep this oil for frying, and clean by sieving it after every use.

Killybegs Fish Pie

Serves 8

Fish pie is a real staple of Irish family cooking and everyone has their own way of making it. This is my version and usually results in lots of very clean plates when it comes to washing up! I named it after the wonderful Donegal port which provides us with most of the fish in the house and restaurant.

Ingredients

12 oz / 350 g haddock fillet
12 oz / 350 g smoked cod fillet
10 oz / 275 g salmon fillet, skin
removed and pin-boned
1 large bay leaf
1¹/₂ pints / 850 ml milk, gently heated
1 lb 12 oz / 800 g floury potatoes,
peeled and cubed

2 tablespoons basil pesto
2 oz / 50 g butter
8 oz / 225 g leeks, thinly sliced
1 small onion, thinly sliced
¹/₄ pint / 150 ml white wine
2 oz / 50 g plain flour
1 tablespoon chopped mixed herbs e.g.
parsley, chives and dill

5 oz / 150 g prawns, cooked
and peeled
2 tablespoons crème fraîche
2 rounded tablespoons
breadcrumbs
Seasoning

Method Preheat the oven to 160°C / Gas 3.

Season the haddock, cod and salmon and place in a roasting tin with the bay leaf and milk. Poach in the oven for 15-20 minutes until the fish flakes easily when tested with a knife. Remove the fish from the tin and take off any remaining skin. Flake the flesh, checking for bones that might have been overlooked. Strain the leftover milk into a measuring jug until you have 1 pint / 570 ml milk (you may need to add in some extra milk if you don't have enough). Discard the bay leaf. Increase the temperature of the oven to 180°C / Gas 4.

Place the potatoes in a large pot of salted water, bring to the boil and cook for 15 minutes until tender. Drain and return to a low heat to dry out a little. Mash the potatoes and beat in half the butter and half the pesto. Season well.

Melt the remaining butter in a small pot and gently cook the leeks and onion for about 5 minutes. Pour in the white wine and reduce by half. Stir in the flour and cook for 1 minute stirring constantly. Gradually pour in the reserved poaching milk and stir until you have a smooth sauce. Season and reduce heat. Add the mixed herbs and simmer for 3 minutes, stirring occasionally. Lastly add the prawns, flaked fish, and crème fraîche and cook for 2 minutes. Be careful not to boil the mixture because the fish will break up and the sauce will go mushy.

Spoon the fish mixture into a shallow ovenproof dish and dot with the remaining pesto. Top it with the mashed potato and sprinkle with the breadcrumbs. Bake in the hot oven for about 20 minutes or until the top is golden brown.

To Serve Place a piping hot portion on a plate or in a bowl - comfort food at its best!

Tip Whenever you're cooking fish, keep end-bits or leftovers and freeze them in a bag. That way, when you come to make this pie, you will already have a selection of fish. Feel free to adapt this recipe to include your own or your family's favourite fish.

Oriental Stir-fry with Toasted Cashews

Serves 4

Everybody's always saying how quick and easy it is to cook a stir-fry, but don't forget that before you start frying, you need to spend a little time getting all the vegetables ready first. That's the real secret to making a stir-fry taste great. This particular dish is handy when you're cooking for vegetarians and non-vegetarians together: simply add in some sautéed chicken pieces after you have served the non-meat eaters.

Ingredients

1 rounded teaspoon Dijon mustard
2 teaspoons honey
2 teaspoons soy sauce
2 oz / 50 g cashew nuts
2 oz / 50 g blanched almonds
2 cloves garlic, thinly sliced
1 teaspoon fresh ginger, cut into strips
1 red chilli, de-seeded & thinly sliced
1 tablespoon sunflower oil

1 red onion, peeled and chopped
1 red and 1 yellow pepper, de-seeded and sliced
1 courgette, cut into sticks or batons
4 oz / 110 g baby corn, halved
4 oz / 110 g mushrooms, quartered
1 packet of egg noodles
1½ oz / 40 g chopped coriander

Method Start by mixing the mustard, honey and soy sauce in a bowl. Then cook the noodles according to packet instructions, drain and keep warm until ready to serve. Now heat the wok for about 1 minute and toss in the cashew nuts and almonds, brown them in the wok for about 2-3 minutes and keep them to one side.

Now raise the heat under the wok, add in the oil and when it is almost smoking, toss in the garlic, ginger and chilli and stir for about 20 seconds. Add the rest of the vegetables and cook on a high heat for about 5 minutes, stirring constantly until golden brown. Add the browned cashews and almonds, and the soy and honey mixture made earlier. Stir for one more minute and finally add 1 oz / 25g of the chopped coriander and season.

To Serve Place the cooked noodles onto the side of a warm plate. Spoon the vegetables beside the noodles and sprinkle with the rest of the chopped coriander.

● **Tip** If you sometimes wonder why your oriental stir-fries don't look like the ones in your takeaway or local restaurant, maybe it's the way you cut your vegetables. Always cut the veg into long thin strips of equal length and you'll be amazed at how authentic it makes them look. When chopping the chilli make sure to clean your hands thoroughly afterwards.

Risotto of Wild Mushrooms and Scallions

Serves 4

The very word risotto seems to strike incredible fear into many a competent cook's heart! I don't know how the rumour got around that risottos were hard to make - they honestly couldn't be easier and I will never stop trying to convince people of that. You just need to use a certain type of fat rice and let it soak up the stock slowly. The most common risotto rice is Arborio and it is easily found in our supermarkets. I promise you, if you make a risotto once, you will never stop making them and trying out all the different variations. But for now, here's an easy one to start you off.

Ingredients

1 oz / 25 g butter
1/2 onion diced
2 cloves garlic, crushed
12 oz / 350 g Arborio rice, or any risotto rice
2 pints / 1.2 litres chicken stock
8 oz / 225 g sliced wild mushrooms: shitake, girolles, chanterelles, oysters

3 scallions, chopped
1 rounded tablespoon chopped basil
1 tablespoon cream
1 oz / 25 g Parmesan shavings
Basil leaves for garnish
Seasoning

Method In a wide-bottomed pot, melt the butter over a medium heat. Sweat the onion and garlic until soft and starting to colour (about 3-4 minutes). Next add the Arborio rice and stir on the heat for 2-3 minutes until all the grains have been coated. Slowly pour in the chicken stock, stirring as you do. Leave the rice to cook over a low heat for about 10 minutes, but stir the pot occasionally during this time.

When the stock has been soaked up, add in the sliced wild mushrooms and simmer for 2-4 minutes, until they have softened. Then add the scallions and basil and stir well. Finally, add in the cream and season to taste.

To Serve Spoon the risotto into a bowl and garnish with some basil leaves and Parmesan shavings made with a vegetable peeler.

Tip When you've mastered this risotto, try out some other fabulous risotto combinations such as pumpkin and red onion or shelled prawns and garden peas. Better still make one up with your own favourite ingredients.

Rigatoni with Chickpea and Tomato Sauce

Serves 6

I love all the different shapes that pasta comes in, but my favourite would have to be rigatoni. The big, ridged shape of this pasta is perfectly suited to this robust sauce. The tomato base is given an extra twist by adding a tin of chickpeas. This gives it a great texture and makes it very nutritious.

Ingredients

2 teaspoons olive oil
1 onion, thinly sliced
1 red pepper, de-seeded and sliced
1 tin chopped tomatoes
1 tin chickpeas, with the liquid
1 bay leaf
1 rounded tablespoon chopped oregano

2 fl oz / 50 ml dry white wine (optional)
1 lb / 450 g rigatoni pasta
(or your preferred shape)
3 oz / 75 g Parmesan, grated
Fresh chives for garnish
Seasoning

Method Heat the olive oil in a pot and gently fry the onion and red pepper for 5 minutes, stirring occasionally until the vegetables are soft. Next, add the tomatoes, chickpeas, bay leaf and the oregano. Add in the wine at this stage, if you are using it. Bring the mixture to the boil stirring constantly and simmer on a low heat until the sauce has reduced. This will take about 10-15 minutes.

While the sauce is simmering, toss the pasta into a large pot of boiling salted water, bring to the boil, stir well and simmer for 6-8 minutes. When the pasta is *al dente*, drain it and keep warm. When the sauce is ready, remove the bay leaf, check seasoning and mix the sauce with the pasta.

To Serve This dish can be served in a large bowl in the centre of the table, or in small bowls for individual portions. Just sprinkle the pasta with Parmesan and chopped chives and garnish with some whole chives.

● Tip There is no doubt that Parmigiano Reggiano (Parmesan) is the undisputed king of Italian cheese, but a lesser-known Italian cheese worth checking out is Pecorino Romano. It is very similar to Parmesan but has a sharper taste and really complements creamy pasta sauces.

Goat's Cheese Puff Pizza with Rocket

Serves 4

Instead of using the normal yeast dough in this pizza, I've made it with puff pastry. This is not as difficult as it sounds because, like a lot of people, I have discovered that you can buy this wonderful pastry ready-made in the frozen-food department of your supermarket. This recipe can be served as 4 individual pizzas or one large pizza.

Ingredients

Packet of puff pastry
1 oz / 25 g butter
1 red pepper, de-seeded and cubed
1 yellow pepper, de-seeded and cubed
1/2 courgette, trimmed and cubed
1/2 aubergine, trimmed and cubed

2 garlic cloves, crushed
2 plum tomatoes, diced
1 teaspoon tomato purée
1 rounded tablespoon chopped basil
1 egg beaten with some milk
3 tablespoons basil pesto

4 oz / 110 g goat's cheese
Basil leaves for garnish
Small bunch of rocket leaves
Seasoning

Method Roll the pastry to a thickness of about 1/4 inch. Place on a baking tray, cover with clingfilm and put in the fridge for at least 30 minutes to rest.

Preheat the oven to 190°C / Gas 5.

First make the vegetable topping by heating the butter in a large frying-pan. Add the peppers, courgettes and aubergines and sauté for 2-3 minutes until they are almost cooked. Check seasoning, set aside and keep warm. In a separate frying-pan cook the garlic, tomatoes, tomato purée and chopped fresh basil and heat gently until the tomatoes go soft. Set aside and keep warm.

Take the pastry out of the fridge and place on a clean chopping board. Cut out four 6-inch / 15cm circles (or a 10-inch / 25 1/2 cm circle if making one pizza). Prick the surface evenly with a fork (this prevents the pastry from bubbling up or rising too much). Replace the pastry on the baking sheet and bake in the oven for 10-15 minutes, until golden brown. Remove pastry from oven, and brush each pizza base with some of the eggwash, to seal the pastry.

To assemble: Spread some tomato sauce on each pizza base, then divide the vegetable mix between the pizzas and spread on top. Crumble some of the goat's cheese on each and drizzle half of the basil pesto sauce over all four pizzas. Put them back in the oven for about 5-10 minutes or until cheese is golden brown.

To Serve Place each pizza on a plate. Garnish with some basil leaves and surround with some rocket leaves. Drizzle the remaining basil pesto on top of the four pizzas.

● Tip The toppings I have used here make this quite a 'posh' pizza, but don't forget the old favourites, especially if you're cooking for children. Choose from a list of pepperoni, mushrooms, pineapple, capers, olives, anchovies, blue cheese, sweetcorn and red Cheddar.

Avocado Spring Rolls with Polenta and Chilli Jam

Serves 4

One of the things I'm often asked is to recommend a vegetarian main course that's good enough to serve at a dinner party. Well, this is one dish that anybody, vegetarian or not, will enjoy. The rolls have a big flavour and look really impressive on the plate.

Ingredients
4 large spring-roll wrappers
1 red onion, diced
4 oz / 110g sun-dried tomatoes, sliced
1 clove garlic, crushed
1 tablespoon basil pesto
1 avocado, peeled, stoned and cubed
1 tablespoon sweet chilli sauce
1 rounded tablespoon chopped herbs
e.g. basil, parsley
1 egg, mixed with 1 tablespoon of milk

Basil leaves for garnish
Frying oil pre-heated to 180˚C / 350˚F

Polenta Discs
1/2 tablespoon olive oil
1 onion, finely diced
1 rounded tablespoon fresh chopped sage
1 1/2 pints / 850 ml vegetable stock
8 oz / 225 g instant polenta
1 tablespoon sweet chilli sauce

Chilli Jam
1 tablespoon olive oil
2 onions, peeled and diced
2 red peppers, de-seeded and diced
1 clove garlic, crushed
1 red chilli, de-seeded
1 tablespoon tomato purée
1 tablespoon balsamic vinegar
2 oz / 50 g brown sugar
4 tomatoes, diced
1 tablespoon dark soy sauce
Seasoning

Method Make the jam by sweating the peppers, onions, garlic and olive oil in a pot over a medium heat for 2 minutes. Stir in the chilli and tomato purée and simmer for 3 more minutes. Now add the vinegar, sugar, tomatoes and soy sauce, cover with cold water and bring to the boil, then simmer for 15-20 minutes. When cooled, blend the mixture in a processor until it forms a purée. Pass this purée through a sieve and check seasoning.

Now for the polenta discs. Put another small pot over a medium heat and cook the onion and sage in the olive oil for 2-3 minutes. Meanwhile boil the vegetable stock in a large pot. Add in the polenta, stirring constantly. Cook for about 7-10 minutes, until it comes away from the sides of the pot. Add the sage, onion and sweet chilli sauce to the polenta and season. Pour the hot wet polenta onto a greased Swiss-roll tin and spread out until about 1/2-inch thick. When it has cooled, cut out 12 discs with a small scone-cutter. Fry the discs in a little olive oil until golden or alternatively you can grill them. Keep warm until ready to serve.

Next make the stuffing. In a frying-pan cook the onion, tomatoes, garlic and pesto over a low heat for 3 minutes. Stir in the avocado, chilli and herbs and simmer for 4-5 minutes. Check the seasoning. Place a spring-roll wrapper on a warm surface and brush the edges with the eggwash. Place some mixture in a sausage shape across the wrapper diagonally. Fold in 3 corners tightly and roll up the rest of the wrapper just as you would with a Swiss roll. Repeat the process for the other 3 spring rolls. Deep-fry for 3-4 minutes and drain on kitchen paper.

To Serve Cut each of the spring rolls into 3, cutting at an angle to give them a nice shape. Place each of them on top of a polenta disc, drizzle with some chilli jam and garnish with some basil, deep fried in the oil.

Tip Don't leave the wrappers lying around the warm kitchen, as they'll dry out and can't be used.

Macaroni, Aubergine and Gruyère Cheese Bake

Serves 4

Feeding the whole family is easy with this versatile bake. Make it in advance and come in from a cold day to a ready-made, hearty dish that's rich in a cheesy sauce. Alternatively, serve this with a fresh crisp salad on a summer evening and it tastes perfect.

Ingredients
1 tablespoon olive oil
1 oz / 25 g butter
1 large aubergine, peeled, trimmed and diced
1 lb / 450 g button mushrooms, quartered
1 lb / 450 g macaroni
12 fl oz / 325 ml cream
1 rounded tablespoon chopped parsley and chives
8 oz / 225 g Gruyère cheese, grated
Chopped parsley for garnish
Seasoning

Method Preheat the oven to 190°C / Gas 5.

Lightly butter a large baking dish with half the butter. Heat the remaining butter with the olive oil in a frying-pan over a high heat. Add the aubergine and mushrooms and sauté for 2-3 minutes until golden brown. Put this mixture into a colander and set aside for the moment.

Bring a large pot of salted water to the boil, add the macaroni and stir well. Bring back to the boil and simmer for about 6-8 minutes. Take the macaroni off when it is *al dente* or still has a little bite to it. Drain well. Put the cream in the empty pasta pot and bring it to the boil. Remove from heat and stir in the parsley and chives. Pour the cooked macaroni into this herb cream, along with the mushrooms, the aubergines and half the Gruyère cheese. Check the seasoning and pour all the ingredients into the buttered baking dish. Sprinkle the remaining cheese on top and bake in the oven for 15 minutes.

To Serve Sprinkle with chopped parsley and bring the bake to the table for serving.

Tip If you are cooking this with children in mind, you might like to substitute white Cheddar cheese for the stronger tasting Gruyère. Try out other favourite vegetables in the sauce e.g. courgette or peppers.

Aromatic Exotic Fruit with Star Anise

Serves 4

Sometimes I like to have something sweet after dinner that is simple and refreshing. So for all cooks who are allergic to pastry-making, mousse-making and sponge-baking, this is the dessert for you: all the flavours you want and none of the hassle.

Ingredients
1 mango, peeled and sliced
$^1/_4$ pineapple, peeled and diced
1 banana, peeled and sliced
2 kiwi fruit, peeled and sliced
$^1/_2$ star fruit, sliced
8 oz / 225 g strawberries, washed, hulled and cut in half
4 fl oz / 110 ml Greek yoghurt
Fresh mint for garnish

Syrup
12 oz / 350 g caster sugar
$^1/_2$ pint / 275 ml pure orange juice
1 vanilla pod, split in half lengthways
5 whole star anise
1 oz / 25 g fresh root ginger, peeled and grated
2 cinnamon sticks
1 lime, juiced

Method To make the syrup, place the sugar and orange juice in a small pot and bring to the boil. Add the remaining syrup ingredients and simmer for 5 minutes. Take off the heat and let the flavours infuse for 20 minutes. Pour the warm syrup onto the prepared fruits and stir well. Leave to cool and store in the fridge.

To Serve Serve cold in a bowl with a dollop of Greek yoghurt and a sprig of mint.

● Tip The basic syrup in this recipe can be made in larger quantities and kept in the fridge in an airtight container. So next time you have leftover fruit you can prepare a quick and easy dessert.

Tiramisu

Serves 8-10

Tiramisu is a traditional Italian dessert and, like a lot of Italian food, we Irish have taken it to our hearts. It's always a popular choice whenever I have it on the restaurant menu.

Ingredients

8 eggs, separated
8 oz / 225 g caster sugar
1 vanilla pod, split in half lengthways
1/2 pint / 275 ml milk
5 gelatine leaves (or 2 sachets of powdered gelatine)
9 oz / 250 g mascarpone cheese
1 pint / 570 ml cream, whipped

2 oz / 50 g best dark chocolate, melted
Raspberries, mint and whipped cream for garnish

Chocolate Sponge
4 eggs
4 oz / 110 g caster sugar
3 oz / 75 g plain flour, sieved

1 oz / 25 g cocoa powder, sieved (plus a little extra for dusting)

Coffee Stock Syrup
4 oz / 110 g caster sugar
1/4 pint / 150 ml water
1 rounded tablespoon coffee
2 tablespoons Tia Maria (or Kahlua)

Method Preheat the oven to 180°C / Gas 4 and line a Swiss-roll tin with greaseproof paper.

First make the chocolate sponge by whisking the eggs and sugar together until thick and pale in colour and the mixture holds a figure of eight when you draw a trail with your whisk. Then fold in the flour and cocoa carefully. Pour the mixture onto the Swiss-roll tin and spread it evenly. Bake in the oven for about 16-20 minutes. Remove from the oven and leave to cool on a wire stand.

Next, make the coffee syrup by simply bringing the water, sugar, coffee and Tia Maria (or Kahlua) to the boil. Stir well and leave to cool. Store in the fridge.

Put the gelatine leaves in a bowl and cover with cold water. Leave to sit for 5 minutes to soften - they will then be very spongy and bend easily. (If you are using powdered gelatine, follow the packet instructions.) While they are softening, make the custard base. Whisk 8 egg yolks and 5 oz / 125g sugar in a bowl until pale. Scrape the seeds from the vanilla pod and stir into the mixture. In a pot, bring the milk just up to the boil and then pour it onto the egg mix, whisking all the time. Pour this mixture back into the pot and simmer on a low heat, stirring continuously until it coats the back of a spoon. Do not boil or the mixture will curdle. Then sieve the custard into a bowl.

Now take the softened gelatine and squeeze out the excess water. Put the sheets into the hot custard and stir until the gelatine has dissolved completely. Whisk in the Mascarpone cheese, sit the bowl over iced or very cold water and keep stirring until it starts to set. Then fold the whipped cream into the custard mixture carefully and set aside. In a separate bowl, whisk 3 egg whites until stiff and slowly add the remaining 3 oz / 75g of caster sugar and continue whisking until it forms stiff peaks. Fold the egg whites into the Mascarpone custard carefully, but thoroughly.

Now assemble the tiramisu. First remove the greaseproof paper from the chocolate sponge, slice the sponge in half diagonally and cover the bottom of a wide dish. Brush all over with the coffee stock syrup and leave to soak for 5 minutes. Pour the Mascarpone custard over the sponge evenly and place in the fridge to set for 3-4 hours or overnight. Finally dust with cocoa powder.

To Serve Drizzle some melted chocolate on a plate. Use a small scone-cutter to make individual tiramisu rounds and transfer to the plate using a fish slice. Garnish with some cream, raspberries and mint.

Classic Lemon Tart

Serves 8

It's said that every chef has his own version of the classic lemon tart and here's mine. It's easy to see why we love it: it's light and tangy with clean bold flavours and colours. I'm serving it here with cream and raspberry sauce, my favourite accompaniment for this dessert.

Ingredients

4 oz / 110 g butter, diced
3 oz / 75 g caster sugar
2 eggs for pastry
9 oz / 250 g plain flour, sieved (plus extra for rolling)
1 whole egg beaten with
1 tablespoon of milk for eggwash

Raspberries, whipped cream and fresh mint for garnish
Baking beans (dried chickpeas, lentils etc will do)

Lemon Filling

5 whole eggs
8 oz / 225 g caster sugar

2 lemons, zest and juice
Plus 2 more lemons, juiced
8 fl oz / 225 ml cream, whipped

Coulis

4 oz / 110 g raspberries
1 rounded teaspoon caster sugar

Method Preheat the oven to 180°C / Gas 4.

To make the pastry, beat the butter and sugar together until light and smooth. Then slowly add in the eggs followed by a tablespoon of the flour and mix thoroughly. Stir in the rest of the flour, using your hands to combine the mixture if necessary. Cover the pastry in clingfilm and place in the fridge for at least 3-4 hours to chill.

For the coulis, blend the raspberries and sugar in the food processor for 1 minute. Pass through a sieve to remove the seeds and keep chilled until ready to serve.

When the pastry is chilled, roll it on a floured counter and line a 9-inch / 23 cm flan ring. Cover the pastry with lightly oiled foil, fill with baking beans and bake blind for 15-20 minutes until the pastry is golden brown. Remove from the oven and take out the foil and baking beans. Brush with the eggwash while the pastry is still warm.

Reduce the oven temperature to 160°C / Gas 3.

Now make the filling. Whisk the 5 eggs, sugar and lemon zest together. Then stir in the lemon juice and fold in the whipped cream. Pour this mixture into the pre-baked pastry case and put in the oven for 25-30 minutes. You'll know the mixture is set when there is a slight 'wobble' to the tart.

To Serve Place a slice of tart on a plate, dot some raspberry coulis to the side of it and garnish with some fresh raspberries and mint. Serve with some lightly whipped cream.

● **Tip** This is a great dinner-party dish and quite a bit can be done in advance to allow you to serve it hot without any fuss. You could make the pastry base the day before and prepare the lemon filling on the day and store it in the fridge. When you want to serve the tart, just add the filling and pop it in the oven 25-30 minutes before you need it. Allow it to cool slightly before serving.

Crème Caramel with Apple Compote

Serves 8

These caramels make a great dinner-party dessert. They look fantastic and the soft vanilla flavour is just the thing after a big meal. But the really great thing about these caramels is that they can be made in advance and kept in the fridge until you're ready to serve.

Ingredients
1 teaspoon oil (for oiling ramekins)
14 fl oz / 385 ml milk
3 fl oz / 75 ml cream
1 vanilla pod
4 whole eggs plus 2 egg yolks
5 oz / 150 g caster sugar
Mint, cream and raspberries to garnish

Caramel Sauce
5 oz / 150 g caster sugar
$^1/_4$ pint / 150 ml water

Apple Compote
1 cooking apple, peeled, cored and cubed
4 oz / 110 g caster sugar
3 fl oz / 75 ml water

Method Lightly oil 8 ramekins (or small teacups). Make the caramel sauce. Place the caster sugar and about a third of the water in a heavy-based pot. Bring to the boil and cook until a deep golden brown. This should take about 15 minutes. When you are happy with the colour, pour the rest of the water into the caramel to stop it from burning. This is a very hot mixture, so be extra careful. Stir the pot continuously until the dark caramel dissolves and the sauce returns to a syrup consistency. Now pour some of the caramel into each of the moulds or teacups.

Preheat the oven to 160°C / Gas 3.

To make the custard put the milk, cream and vanilla pod into a saucepan and bring to the boil. Remove immediately from the heat and set aside. In a separate bowl, whisk the 4 eggs with the 2 egg yolks and the caster sugar. Take the vanilla pod from the saucepan, split it in half and scrape the seeds into the egg mixture. Now pour the hot milk onto the eggs, whisking constantly. Pour the custard through a sieve into a bowl.

With a soup ladle, gently fill the ramekins (or small teacups) right up to the rim. Place in a deep baking tray, half-filled with cold water. This is called a 'bain-marie'. Put the tray in the oven for 30-40 minutes. The mixture will be slightly 'wobbly' when set. Leave the ramekins to cool in the tray and then transfer them to the fridge until ready to serve.

For the apple compote, place the sugar and water in a pot and bring to the boil. Add the cubed apples and bring back to the boil. Using a slotted spoon, remove the apples from the pot immediately and leave to cool.

To Serve Turn the crème caramel out of the ramekin or teacup and onto a chilled plate, making sure you get all the caramel out. Spoon the apples around it. Garnish with a raspberry, some mint and cream.

●**Tip** Cooking in a bain-marie is vital for this dish as it prevents the custard from curdling. It is important that the caramels are cooked very slowly and the water does not boil. Run a knife around the inside of the ramekins or teacups to help remove the crème caramels.

Passion Fruit Pavlova with Raspberries

Serves 4

This is a stunning finale to any meal. You can make either one large pavlova or 4 small individual ones. This tastes best in late summer or early autumn when the raspberries are sweet and luscious.

Ingredients

Meringue
4 egg whites
8 oz / 225 g caster sugar
1 vanilla pod, seeds only
8 oz / 225 g fresh raspberries
2 oz / 50 g best white chocolate, grated
Fresh mint for garnish

Passion Fruit Curd
2 whole eggs plus 2 egg yolks
(use yolks from meringue eggs)
4 oz / 110 g sugar
2 lemons, zest of 1 and juice of 2
4 passion fruit, seeds only
4 oz / 110 g unsalted butter, diced
3 fl oz / 75 ml cream, whipped

Raspberry Coulis
1 oz / 25 g sugar
1 fl oz / 25 ml water
4 oz / 110 g fresh raspberries

Method Preheat the oven to 100°C / Gas ¼.

Whisk 4 egg whites until stiff and then gradually add in the caster sugar and the vanilla seeds. Whisk until the whites become thick and glossy and form stiff peaks (and if you turn the bowl upside down the mix won't fall out). Using a piping-bag or knife, spread the mixture onto an oven tray lined with silicone paper and cook in the oven for 3-4 hours. Do use silicone paper as the meringue can stick to greaseproof paper and will break easily when you try to remove it.

For the curd, put the eggs, the egg yolks and the sugar in a bowl over a pot of simmering water and whisk until the mixture is a pale colour and keeps a figure of eight shape when made with the whisk. Stir in the lemon zest, lemon juice and passion fruit seeds and cook for 15-20 minutes until it starts to set. It is important not to let the water boil under the bowl as this will curdle the eggs. Remove the bowl from the pot and leave to cool for about 15-20 minutes. Whisk in the diced butter until combined, and leave the curd to cool. Finally, fold in the whipped cream and keep chilled until ready to serve.

To make the raspberry coulis put the sugar and water in a pan and bring to the boil. Leave bubbling for 2-3 minutes and remove from heat for 20 minutes. When cool, add the raspberries and blend in a mixer for about 1-2 minutes. Pass through a sieve to remove seeds and keep cool.

To Serve Spread the curd on the meringue and fill with the fresh red fruit. Drizzle the coulis around the meringue and garnish with grated white chocolate and mint.

●Tip As meringue cases keep for weeks in an airtight container, why not double up the quantities so that you always have some in the house for a quick dessert.

Strawberry Yoghurt Mousse

Serves 6

Strawberry and vanilla are simply glorious together but this dish can be made with any other flavoured yoghurt. This is a lovely light dessert to finish off a meal and will suit you if you are watching your waistline.

Ingredients

Mousse
3 eggs, separated
4 oz / 110 g caster sugar
1 vanilla pod, seeds only
1/4 pint / 150 ml milk
5 gelatine leaves (or 2 sachets powdered gelatine)
1/4 pint / 150 ml strawberry yoghurt

4 fl oz / 110 ml cream, whipped
1 tablespoon sunflower oil
6 sprigs fresh mint

Strawberry & Mango Salsa
1 ripe mango, peeled and diced
6 strawberries, washed, hulled and diced
1 tablespoon orange juice

Method Whisk 3 egg yolks with 3 oz of the sugar until the mixture thickens. In a pot bring the milk and the vanilla seeds to the boil. Pour the hot milk onto the egg yolks, whisking continuously. Transfer this custard back into the pot and cook on low heat until the mixture thickens and will coat the back of a spoon. Do not allow the mixture to boil, as it will curdle very easily. Pass the custard through a sieve into a clean bowl.

Next soak the gelatine in water for 5 minutes or until it is soft and bends easily. Then drain off the excess water and add the gelatine to the warm custard, stirring constantly until it has completely dissolved. (If you are using powdered gelatine, follow the packet instructions.) Now place the bottom of the bowl into iced or very cold water. Leave for about 15-20 minutes or until semi-set around the edges. Then whisk in the strawberry yoghurt and whipped cream until fully combined.

Next whisk the 3 egg whites until they double in volume. Gradually add the remaining caster sugar until the egg whites are glossy and form stiff peaks. Gently fold the egg whites into the yoghurt custard taking care not to overmix. Pour this mixture into lightly oiled ramekins (or small teacups) and leave to set for at least 3-4 hours or preferably overnight.

For the salsa, simply mix the mango, strawberries and orange juice and leave the flavours to infuse.

To Serve Dip base of each ramekin (or teacup) in warm water to help dislodge the mousse. Tip the mousse onto a plate and serve with some strawberry and mango salsa and garnish with a sprig of mint.

● **Tip** While this recipe conveniently uses 3 egg yolks and 3 egg whites, sometimes you might find that a dessert recipe calls for 3 or 4 egg whites only and no yolks or vice versa. So I always keep leftover egg whites in a cup in the fridge, where they last a week. As the yolks freeze so well, I put leftover yolks in a small container in the freezer.

Apple Crumble with Cinnamon and Walnuts

Serves 6-8

Everyone's favourite, the apple tart. This is my version of that famous Irish classic. I've added nuts for extra texture and a bit of cinnamon in the crumble for flavour. I like to make this in small individual tins because it looks so amazing on the plate. But you can use a large tin to save time and serve more people.

Ingredients

Pastry
4 oz / 110 g butter, diced
3 oz / 75 g icing sugar
9 oz / 250 g plain flour
(plus a little extra for rolling)
1 egg

Filling
4 large Bramley apples, peeled,
cored and cubed

4 oz / 110 g caster sugar
1 tablespoon lemon juice
1/2 pint / 275 ml water

Crumble
4 oz / 110 g butter
6 oz / 175 g plain flour
4 oz / 110 g brown sugar
2 oz / 50 g walnuts, chopped
1 teaspoon ground cinnamon

Caramel Sauce
10 oz / 275 g caster sugar
1/4 pint / 150 ml water
8 fl oz / 225 ml cream
3 oz / 75g butter

Method First make the pastry by creaming the butter and icing sugar together. Slowly add the egg and flour and mix well. Cover with clingfilm and leave in the fridge to relax for at least 3 hours. This pastry is very sticky and has a 'cake-like' texture, so chilling is vital before rolling. When ready, roll the pastry on a floured counter and line six 4-inch / 10cm tartlet tins (or a 9-inch / 23 cm tart tin). Rest in the fridge for about 1 hour.

Now for the filling. Boil the sugar, water and lemon juice in a pot. Add the apples and bring to the boil. Remove apples immediately using a slotted spoon. Leave to cool.

Preheat the oven to 190˚C / Gas 5.

To make the crumble, rub the butter and flour together lightly. Add the sugar, cinnamon and walnuts and mix together well. Spoon the cooled apples into the tartlet tins. Sprinkle the crumble mixture over them and bake in the oven for 20 minutes, or until the top is golden brown.

To make the caramel sauce, place the sugar and water in a heavy-bottomed pot. Bring to the boil and cook for approximately 15 minutes or until it has a golden-brown colour (if it's too dark it will become bitter). Stir in the cream and butter and mix well. Keep on the heat until it reaches a thick sauce consistency. Leave to cool and store in the fridge. This sauce will keep for up to two weeks.

To Serve Place individual tarts onto plate and serve with ice cream and caramel sauce.

● Tip Whenever I do an apple pie or apple crumble on *Open House*, we get inundated with requests for the recipe, so I know this will be a winner in your home. Take advantage of the seasons to adapt the above recipe. In the autumn blackberry and apple make a great combination and in summer try using an apple and strawberry version.

Bailey's Cheesecake with Pineapple Caramel Sauce

Serves 8-10

Everyone should have a good cheesecake recipe; it keeps well and can be frozen. I've incorporated Bailey's liqueur into mine, because the soft flavour complements a cheesecake perfectly. This dessert will serve 8 if made in individual tins or 10 if you make 1 large cheesecake.

Ingredients
2 oz / 50 g margarine
5 oz / 150 g digestive biscuits, crumbled
2 oz / 50 g best dark chocolate, melted
1 packet of dried pineapple crisps for garnish
8 x 4-inch / 10 cm tartlet tins (or 10-inch / 25$^{1}/_{2}$ cm springform tin)

Bailey's Topping
4 drops pure vanilla extract
8 fl oz / 225 ml milk
4 eggs separated
5 oz / 150 g caster sugar
5 leaves gelatine (or 2 sachets of powdered gelatine)
10 oz / 275 g cream cheese
2 tablespoons Bailey's Irish Cream
$^{1}/_{4}$ pint / 150 ml cream, lightly whipped

Pineapple Caramel Sauce
4 oz / 110 g caster sugar
$^{1}/_{4}$ pint / 150 ml water
$^{1}/_{4}$ pint / 150 ml pineapple juice
$^{1}/_{2}$ vanilla pod
1 oz / 25 g pineapple, diced

Method First make the base by melting the margarine and pouring it onto the crumbled digestive biscuits. Stir well, press into the base of the individual tartlet tins (or one large tin) and leave to set in the fridge. Then soak the gelatine leaves in cold water for 5 minutes. When ready they will be soft and flexible. (If you are using powdered gelatine, follow the packet instructions.)

Next make the topping by boiling the milk and vanilla extract in a pot. In a bowl, whisk the egg yolks and 4 oz / 100 g of sugar until it is pale and fluffy. Next pour the milk onto the eggs, whisking constantly. Pour the mixture back into the pot and cook on a low heat. Stir until it coats the back of a spoon and do not allow it to boil or it will curdle. Finally pass the custard through a sieve into a clean bowl.

Drain off the water from the gelatine and stir into the warm custard until dissolved. Place the bottom of the bowl of custard into some iced or very cold water and leave until semi-set around the edges. In a separate bowl, whisk the cheese and Bailey's until the mixture is smooth and pale in colour, then fold into the custard. Lastly fold the whipped cream into the custard carefully.

In a separate bowl, whisk the egg whites until they double in volume. Gradually add the remaining 1 oz / 25g sugar and whisk until it is glossy and forms peaks. Carefully fold the egg whites into the custard. Now pour the mixture onto the biscuit base in the tartlet tins and flatten with a spatula or palette knife and leave to set in the fridge for 4-5 hours or overnight.

For the sauce, place the sugar and water in a saucepan and cook until a golden caramel colour. Stir in the pineapple juice, followed by the vanilla pod and diced pineapple. Leave for about 5 minutes on a gentle heat until it has a sauce consistency, remove the vanilla pod and then cool.

To Serve Take each cheesecake from the tartlet tin carefully. Drizzle melted chocolate over the top and serve with whipped cream and the cold pineapple caramel sauce and garnish with a pineapple crisp.

● **Tip** Nowadays, nearly all supermarkets stock gelatine. I prefer to use leaf gelatine, which most good food shops stock. But you can use powdered gelatine if you prefer.

Leg of Spring Lamb with a Mint Mash

Serves 8-10

Easter heralds the spring and with it the start of the lamb season. This is a dish traditionally eaten in Ireland over the Easter holiday, when the lamb is at its best. This simple recipe is one all the family will enjoy.

Ingredients
4 - 4$^{1}/_{2}$ lb / 1.8 - 2 kg leg of lamb
2 large sprigs of rosemary
3 cloves garlic, peeled and sliced
2 lb / 900 g potatoes, peeled
2 lb / 900 g carrots, peeled and cut into wedges
2 oz / 50 g butter
1 tablespoon milk
2 teaspoons shop-bought mint sauce
Fresh mint for garnish
Seasoning

Home-made Mint Sauce
$^{1}/_{4}$ pint / 150 ml malt vinegar
Small bunch of mint leaves, chopped
2 rounded tablespoons brown sugar

Method Preheat the oven to 200°C / Gas 6.

Using a sharp knife, make small incisions in the lamb and press a garlic slice and some rosemary well into each slit. Weigh the joint, and allow 20 minutes cooking time per 1lb / 450 g plus an extra 20 minutes. Place the lamb in a roasting tray and cook for 20 minutes then reduce the oven temperature to 180°C / Gas 4 for the rest of the cooking time. If you don't like your lamb too pink in the middle, add 20 more minutes to the cooking time.

Cook half the potatoes in boiling salted water for about 20 minutes and drain. Add the butter and milk to the potatoes and mash until creamy. Stir the shop-bought mint sauce into the potato and season to taste. Keep warm until ready to serve.

Meanwhile, place the mint in a saucepan, pour the vinegar over it and add the sugar. Bring to the boil and cook for 3 minutes until the sugar has dissolved. Set aside and keep for serving.

40 minutes before the end of the roasting time take out the lamb. Add the carrots and the rest of the potatoes to the tray, baste the meat with the juices and return to the oven. When time is up, remove the lamb and vegetables from the tray. Allow the lamb to rest for about 15 minutes before carving.

To Serve Place the lamb on a large dish, surrounded by the roast potatoes and carrots. Place the mint mash in a bowl with a garnish of fresh mint and serve with the home-made mint sauce on the side.

● **Tip** Sometimes when you're cooking a joint, especially an expensive piece of meat like this one, you need to sit down with a pen and paper and work out weights and timings etc. So take a moment to calculate everything in your own time.

Honey-roasted Duck with Red Cabbage and Apple

Serves 2-4

The first thing you should know about duck is that its size is very deceptive. What looks like a large duck will probably feed only 2 hungry people or 4 with smaller portions. The cavity is quite big and there is a lot of fat to be rendered off. But when you get over those drawbacks, duck is a rich, succulent meat that really wakes a jaded palate.

Ingredients
2$^1/_2$ - 3lb / 1-1.3 kg oven-ready duck
1 rounded teaspoon peppercorns, crushed
1 rounded teaspoon coarse sea salt
5 tablespoons clear honey
Small bunch of fresh thyme

Red Cabbage and Apple
1 tablespoon vegetable oil
1 head red cabbage, finely sliced
2 tablespoons balsamic vinegar
4 rounded tablespoons brown sugar
$^1/_2$ pint / 275 ml red wine
$^1/_2$ pint / 275 ml apple juice

2 cooking apples, peeled, cored and chopped
2 tablespoons raisins
1 rounded teaspoon ground cinnamon
1 rounded teaspoon mixed spice
1 rounded teaspoon ground cloves
Seasoning

Method Preheat the oven to 160°C / Gas 3.

Place the duck on a small roasting tray and lightly score the breast about 6 or 7 times, just cutting into the skin. Then push the salt and peppercorns right into the flesh. Spread the honey over the duck, making sure it's skin is completely coated, and put the duck in the oven to slow roast for 2$^1/_2$ hours. Baste the duck with the juices every 20 minutes.

To prepare the cabbage and apple, heat the oil in a heavy-bottomed pot and add the cabbage, vinegar, sugar, wine and apple juice. Cover with a lid and simmer for 1 hour over a low heat. Next stir in the apples, raisins and spices and cook gently for another 30 minutes until soft. Lastly add seasoning and check whether the mixture needs more sugar.

When the 2$^1/_2$ hours are up, remove the duck from the oven, and the tray, and leave to rest for 15 minutes. If the honey juices in the tray are still runny, then place the tray on the stove-top and heat for 5 minutes or until the juices have a sauce consistency. Then pour the juices over the duck and leave to rest for another 15 minutes.

To Serve Put the cabbage and apple mixture on a large heated serving dish. Place the duck on top and garnish with fresh thyme.

●Tip You'll find you have lots and lots of duck fat with this recipe. Don't throw it away - keep it in the fridge, as it is fantastic for frying vegetables and, of course, for roasting potatoes. You could use it for my duck confit recipe also.

Breaded Bacon Chops with a Bushmills Sauce

Serves 4

It's always good to break out the traditional fare when you have guests from abroad eating with you. This is what we serve visiting relatives and friends. They love to taste authentic Irish food and there's nothing as Irish as "bacon and cabbage"!

Ingredients
1 lb / 450 g loin of bacon
1 egg beaten with some milk
1 rounded tablespoon seasoned plain flour
4 oz / 110 g white breadcrumbs
3 oz / 75 g butter
1 fl oz / 25 ml olive oil
4 slices fresh pineapple

1/4 head Savoy or York cabbage, sliced
Seasoning

Whiskey Sauce
8 fl oz / 225 ml water
4 oz / 110 g sugar
2 tablespoons Bushmills (or any whiskey)

Method Place the bacon in a pot of cold unsalted water and bring to the boil. If the water is still very salty, repeat this process. Then simmer the bacon on a medium heat for a further 30 minutes, or until a skewer stuck in the meat has just a little 'give' to it. Take the bacon from the pot and drain well. Trim off any excess fat, cut the bacon into 4 chops and dry with kitchen paper. Dip each chop in the seasoned flour, shaking off the excess. Then dip the chops into the egg mixture and finally cover the chops with the breadcrumbs, making sure they are coated thoroughly. Set aside for now.

Now make the whiskey sauce by putting the sugar and water in a saucepan and bringing to the boil. Keep the heat on and wait until it is a deep golden colour. This should take about 8-10 minutes, but stay nearby as it happens very quickly and do be careful as this sauce is very hot. When the colour is deep enough add the whiskey. It'll steam up and then cool into a thick lumpy sauce. Keep on a low heat stirring until the sauce becomes smooth.

Place the pineapple rings under a hot grill until the juices caramelise and the pineapple browns. Keep warm until serving. Next prepare the cabbage. Heat 1 oz / 25g of butter in a large frying-pan over a moderate heat. Stir in the cabbage and a tablespoon of water and fry for 4 minutes until soft. Season to taste.

To fry the chops, heat the olive oil and the remaining butter in another frying-pan. Fry both sides of the chops until golden.

To Serve Lay out the chops in a fan shape on a large heated serving dish. Place the cabbage and the pineapple rings alongside, and drizzle with the Bushmills sauce.

●Tip This basic caramel sauce will keep in the fridge for weeks in an airtight container. If you want a plain sweet caramel sauce, just substitute the same quantity of cold water for the whiskey to stop the caramelising.

Roast Sirloin of Beef with Red Wine Gravy

Serves 8-10

Well, there's no denying it, a roast beef lunch isn't cheap. But when you're making a special effort, it never fails to please the family. If you follow this recipe, you'll have the roast you want, the way you want it, and you can sit back and watch the family enjoy it.

Ingredients
6 lb / 2.7 - 3 kg sirloin of beef
2 fl oz / 50 ml olive oil
4 shallots, peeled and halved
2 cloves garlic, halved
3 sprigs thyme
12 fl oz / 350 ml red wine
1/2 pint / 275 ml beef stock
Pinch of sugar (optional)
Seasoning

Parsnip and Potato Mash
1lb / 450 g peeled parsnips,
cut into cubes
1lb / 450 g peeled potatoes,
cut into cubes
2 fl oz / 50 ml cream
Pinch of grated nutmeg
2 oz / 50 g butter

Horseradish Sauce
2 oz / 50 g fresh horseradish,
finely grated
1 teaspoon Dijon mustard
1 tablespoon white wine vinegar
1 rounded teaspoon caster sugar
1/2 pint / 275 ml whipping cream

Method Preheat the oven to 190°C / Gas 5.

Put the oil in a roasting tray and place on a high heat on the stove-top. Season the beef all over and when the oil is very hot place the beef on the roasting tray. Cook for about 2 minutes to seal in the juices, then turn the sirloin over and do the same on the other side. Cover the top of the joint with foil and put in the oven for 15 minutes per 1 lb / 450 g if you like your beef medium rare. For a medium finish, cook for 15 minutes longer and add another 10 minutes to the cooking time for well-done beef. Baste the beef with the tray juices every 15 minutes to ensure all-round flavour. Halfway through the cooking time, turn the meat over and add the shallots, garlic and thyme.

While the meat is cooking, prepare the mash by putting the parsnips and potatoes in a large pot. Cover with water and bring to the boil, then simmer until tender (about 25-30 minutes). Drain and keep warm. Meanwhile, in a saucepan, bring the cream to the boil and add the nutmeg. Add this creamy mixture to the parsnip and potatoes and check for seasoning. Toss in the butter and liquidise or blend until smooth. Keep warm until ready to serve.

To make the horseradish, place all the ingredients in a bowl and whisk together vigorously until it has the consistency of lightly whipped cream. Then it is ready. Keep chilled until serving.

Once the meat is cooked, take it out of the oven and remove from the roasting tray. Cover the beef with foil and leave to rest for 20 minutes before carving. Leave the shallots, garlic and thyme in the tray and reheat on the cooker. Add the wine and reduce by half, then add the stock and reduce until thick. Adjust the seasoning and sieve the juices. The gravy is ready. If you find the taste too sharp just add the pinch of sugar.

To Serve Place on a large heated dish and serve with the parsnip and potato mash and the home-made horseradish.

Tip We rarely have any leftovers when it comes to a roast beef dinner. But if you do, why not use it to make the tastiest sandwiches as a treat? Use nice rustic or country bread, a little home-made horseradish and some crispy lettuce.

Roast Free-range Chicken with Herb Butter

Serves 4-6

For some reason, people don't seem to want chicken legs as much as breasts, but this recipe will have everyone fighting for the legs. By slitting the chicken thighs and infusing the meat with delicious herbs, people will realise they have under-estimated the meat on the humble drumstick!

Ingredients
3 lb / 1.4 kg free-range chicken
1 lemon, halved
1 bay leaf
2 sprigs of rosemary
4 whole cloves garlic, peeled
2 oz / 50 g chopped herbs e.g. basil, parsley and tarragon
2 fl oz / 50 ml olive oil
Seasoning

Bread Sauce
1 onion, studded with 2-3 whole cloves
4 black peppercorns
1 bay leaf
Pinch of nutmeg
$1/2$ pint / 275 ml milk
2oz / 50 g white breadcrumbs

Method Preheat the oven to 200°C / Gas 6.

Wash the chicken inside and out and dry as much as possible with kitchen paper. (You can remove the wishbone if you want to as this will help when you carve the chicken.) Next rub the cavity with salt and then stuff it with the lemon, bay leaf, rosemary and garlic.

Take a piece of skin at the tip of the breast and pull it away from the flesh and with your hand loosen it gently along the whole chicken, so that there is a pocket between the raw skin and the chicken flesh. Push half the herbs into this pocket, making sure you get right along the breast. Rub the flesh with half the oil and then pull the skin back over the herbed flesh.

Now slash the meat on each chicken leg 3 times with a knife and rub the rest of the herbs and the remaining olive oil into the flesh. Season the chicken and place on a roasting tray. Bend the winglets back and tuck underneath the bird. Cook for $1 1/2$ -2 hours, reducing the oven temperature to 180°C / Gas 4 after 20 minutes. If you have a very large chicken you may need to leave it in a little longer.

Make the bread sauce by putting the onion, peppercorns, bay leaf and nutmeg in a small heated pot. Pour in the milk and bring to the boil. Remove from the heat and leave to infuse for 30-40 minutes. Take out the onion, peppercorns and bay leaf, add the breadcrumbs and cook on a low heat for 15 minutes or until the sauce has thickened. Keep the sauce warm until ready to serve.

To Serve Place the chicken on a large heated serving dish and carve at the table for maximum effect. Serve sauce in a bowl.

Tip Always check that the juices of a chicken run clear before removing from the oven. Do this by pressing the point of a knife into the leg and releasing some juice.

Roast Ham with Balsamic and Mustard Glaze

Serves 10-14

Christmas Day is the only day of the year that my whole family gets together and has a feast. We always make sure that our mum, Vera, puts her feet up that day. So, I generally take on ham-making duties. But Christmas wouldn't be Christmas if we didn't use my mother's fabulous balsamic-and-mustard ham glaze.

Ingredients
10 lb / 4¹/₂ kg knuckle-end gammon, soaked in cold water overnight and then drained
2 carrots, halved
2 sticks celery, halved
2 onions, peeled and halved
4 bay leaves
12 peppercorns

Glaze
8 cloves
1 rounded tablespoon English mustard
1 rounded teaspoon ground ginger
¹/₄ pint / 150 ml Golden Syrup
1 tablespoon balsamic (or other good) vinegar
4 oz / 110 g brown sugar

Cranberry Sauce
1 lb / 450 g cranberries
4 oz / 110 g brown sugar
Pinch cinnamon
2 oranges, peeled and chopped
3 spring onions, chopped
Dash Tabasco sauce
Seasoning

Method Place the gammon in a pot of water with the carrots, celery, onions, bay leaves and peppercorns. Bring to the boil and simmer for 20 minutes per 1lb / 450g, plus 20 minutes extra. When cooked remove from the pot and allow the ham to cool. Now trim off some of the excess skin and fat and score with a sharp knife.

Preheat the oven to 180°C / Gas 4.

Mix the mustard and ginger and rub all over the gammon. Push the cloves into the skin randomly. Place the joint on a large roasting-pan or baking dish. Mix the Golden Syrup with the vinegar and brush this all over the meat. Sprinkle with the sugar and bake in the oven for 40-45 minutes. Spoon the pan juices over the joint at regular intervals. When cooked, remove from the oven and leave to rest for 10-15 minutes.

To make the sauce, place all the ingredients in a small pan and simmer gently for 20 minutes over a low heat, stirring occasionally. Keep warm until ready to serve.

To Serve Place a slice of the glazed ham on the plate and garnish with the cranberry sauce.

Tip There's always ham left over after Christmas. My favourite way to use it is to heat a pitta bread in the toaster. Open the pitta and stick in a thick slice of ham, one grilled pineapple slice and some cheese. It all melts together in the hot bread and it's delicious.

Roast Thornhill Turkey with Walnut Stuffing

Serves 8-12

I'm so lucky to live in a small village like Blacklion, and yet to have one of the best poultry farmers in the country just 5 minutes away from our house. All year I get all my free-range chickens and ducks there and come Christmas I can wander up the road to get the best turkey and goose in the country.

Ingredients
12 lb / 5½ kg turkey
8 oz / 225 g white breadcrumbs
4 oz / 110 g porridge oats
2 rounded tablespoons chopped parsley
1 rounded teaspoon rosemary and chopped sage

3 oz / 75 g walnuts, chopped
4 oz / 110g fresh or dried cranberries
1 orange, rind and juice
1 egg, beaten
6 fl oz / 175 ml butter, melted

Gravy
1 tablespoon plain flour
3 tablespoons port or red wine
3 sprigs of thyme
1 pint / 570 ml chicken stock
Seasoning

Method Preheat the oven to 190°C / Gas 5.

Start by making the stuffing. Place the breadcrumbs, oats, herbs, walnuts and cranberries into a bowl and season. Add the orange rind, orange juice, 4 fl oz / 110ml of the melted butter, and the beaten egg. Mix thoroughly. Lift the flap at the neck of the turkey and place the stuffing into that cavity, making sure you push it down well. When full, pull the flap back over the neck and secure with cocktail sticks. (If you need extra stuffing, double the quantities and shape half of it into a sausage shape, cover with tinfoil and bake beside the turkey.)

Turn the turkey breast-side up, pull the turkey feet close together at the top of the bird and tie with some string or elastic (this allows for a dramatic presentation). Now weigh the turkey to calculate the required cooking time. You will need approximately 20-25 minutes per 1lb / 450 g. Add on an extra 20 minutes and allow 10 more minutes for resting the bird.

Place the turkey in a large roasting-tin, brush the skin all over with the remaining butter and season well. Loosely cover the top of the turkey in foil, leaving air to circulate around it, and put in the oven. After 1½ hours reduce the oven temperature to 180°C / Gas 4. Make sure to baste the turkey by spooning juices from the roasting-tin over it every 40 minutes. Take off the foil for the final 40 minutes to get the skin crispy. When cooking time is up, remove the turkey from the oven and push the point of a knife into the leg of the turkey. If the juices run clear you'll know the meat is ready. Transfer to a warm plate and remove the strings. Cover with foil and leave to rest. (Slice any extra stuffing you have into little rounds for garnish.)

While the turkey is resting, make the gravy by heating the juices in the roasting tin over a gentle heat on the stove top. Slowly whisk in the flour and cook for 2 minutes. Add the port or red wine, the thyme and finally the stock, bring to the boil and leave to simmer for 10 minutes, stirring occasionally. The gravy is ready when the sauce has reduced and thickened to your preference. Pass through a sieve and season to taste.

To Serve Serve on a large warmed oval dish with herbs and extra stuffing arranged around the meat.

● Tip I know it sounds obvious, but do check the size of your oven before going out to get your turkey. You'd be amazed at the number of people who can't fit the whole turkey into the oven on Christmas morning. Be sure to leave plenty of room for the heat to circulate around the bird.

MacNean Traditional Christmas Cake

This is a very special recipe that has been handed down the Maguire family for generations. My Auntie Maureen was kind enough to let me share this with you all and I hope your family enjoy it as much as we do every Christmas.

Ingredients

14 oz / 400 g raisins
14 oz / 400 g sultanas
6 oz / 175 g currants
4 oz / 110 g cherries
4 oz / 110 g mixed peel, home-made or similar
2 oz / 50 g grated apple
2 oz / 50 g apricots, ready to eat and chopped

$1/2$ teaspoon nutmeg, grated
$1/4$ teaspoon mixed spice
$1/2$ teaspoon cinnamon
2 oz / 50 g chopped almonds
$1/2$ lemon rind, grated
$1/2$ pint / 150 ml whiskey

8 oz / 225 g butter
8 oz / 225 g soft brown sugar
6 eggs, beaten
10 oz / 275 g plain flour, sieved
2 oz / 50 g ground almonds

Method   Preheat the oven to 140°C / Gas 1.

Prepare a 9 inch / 23 cm round cake tin by lining with 2 layers of greaseproof paper extending 2 inches over top of the tin. Tie a double band of brown paper around the outside of the tin.

In a large bowl place the raisins, sultanas, currants, cherries, mixed peel, apple, apricots, nutmeg, mixed spice, cinnamon, chopped almonds, lemon rind and $1/2$ of whiskey. Mix thoroughly and cover the bowl with a tea towel and leave overnight.

Cream the butter and sugar until light and fluffy. Add the beaten eggs and sieved flour and beat until well mixed. Mix in the soaked fruit and the ground almonds and mix well. Put the mixture into the prepared tin and smooth with the back of a spoon leaving a slight hollow in the centre.

Bake the cake for 3-$3^1/2$ hours. Protect the top of cake from over-browning by covering with brown paper for the last $1^1/2$ hours of baking. As oven temperatures can vary, check the cake after $1^1/2$-2 hours. Test by inserting a small skewer into the centre of the cake – when it comes out dry the cake is ready.

Cool the cake in the tin until next day. Then turn it out and remove the paper. Using a skewer, make about 8 small holes in the cake and pour the remaining whiskey over it. Wrap the cake in 2 sheets of greaseproof paper and then cover with a layer of foil. Store in an airtight tin in a cool place.

● Tip I haven't included icing in this recipe, because personally I like my cake plain. However, there are so many different types of icing around (e.g. fondant, royal), I'll leave you to choose your own favourite. This cake should be made at least 1 month in advance.

MacNean Special Christmas Pudding

Another Auntie Maureen classic! This pudding is a dense, rich and utterly mouth-watering dessert. In fact it's so rich that I serve it with lightly whipped cream and not the traditional brandy butter. Of course, you can serve it with either. I always make the Christmas Pudding 4-6 weeks in advance to allow the flavours to

Ingredients

2 oz / 50 g plain flour	2 oz / 50 g currants	1 lemon, rind and juice
1/2 teaspoon mixed spice	6 oz / 175 g sultanas	6 oz / 175 g butter, melted
1/2 teaspoon grated nutmeg	2 oz / 50 g mixed peel	2 eggs, beaten
1/2 teaspoon ground cloves	2 oz / 50 g chopped almonds	1/4 pint / 150 ml Guinness
6 oz / 175 g breadcrumbs	1/2 apple, diced	8 fl oz / 225 ml whipped cream
6 oz / 175 g soft brown sugar	1/2 small carrot, grated	2 x 2 pint / 1.2 litre pudding bowls
6 oz / 175 g raisins		

Method Sift together flour, mixed spice, nutmeg and cloves. Add the breadcrumbs, sugar, raisins, currants, sultanas, mixed peel, almonds, apple, carrot, lemon rind, lemon juice and melted butter and mix until well combined. Add the beaten eggs gradually, stirring constantly, followed by the Guinness. Mix everything thoroughly and cover with a tea towel and leave overnight.

Preheat the oven to 150˚C / Gas 2.

Place the mixture in the pudding bowls. Wrap the bowls with greaseproof paper and seal with the lids. (If you don't have lids for your bowls, wrap them completely in tinfoil instead.) To cook the pudding, stand in a large cake tin and fill the tin 3/4 full of boiling water. Cover the tin with foil.

Bake in the oven for 7 hours. Allow to cool. Cover the pudding bowls again with greaseproof paper and store in a cool dry place. On Christmas day, remove the extra greaseproof paper and bake your pudding as before, by placing it in a cake tin 3/4 full of boiling water for 2-3 hours.

To Serve Place in a bowl or on a plate, with a dollop of lightly whipped cream.

Tip If you must light the pudding, do please be careful with the amount of alcohol you pour on. I find that 1 tablespoon of heated brandy works just fine.

MacNean Old-fashioned Mincemeat Pies

Makes 12

Not surprisingly, my Auntie Maureen is also the champion of this Maguire classic. Before she retired she was a Domestic Science teacher and I don't believe she ever had a pupil who didn't learn how to make her marvellous mincemeat pies. Once you've made mincemeat yourself, you'll never buy another jar of the stuff again. This recipe will fill 5-6 regular sized jamjars.

Ingredients
Sweet Pastry
8 oz / 225 g plain flour (plus extra for rolling)
2 oz / 50 g icing sugar
5 oz / 150 g butter or margarine, diced
1 egg yolk
1 tablespoon cold water
$^{1}/_{2}$ teaspoon lemon juice
1 egg, beaten for glaze
Jar of mincemeat (bought or home-made)
Tartlet tin for 12 pies

Mincemeat
12 oz / 350 g eating apples, peeled, cored and diced
8 oz / 225 g raisins
8 oz / 225 g sultanas
8 oz / 225 g currants
4 oz / 110 g candied citrus peel
8 oz / 225 g butter, melted
4 oz / 110 g blanched almonds, chopped
6 oz / 175 g dark brown sugar
1 orange, rind grated
1 lemon, rind grated
$^{1}/_{2}$ teaspoon grated nutmeg
$^{1}/_{2}$ teaspoon ground cinnamon
$^{1}/_{2}$ teaspoon ground cloves
$^{1}/_{2}$ teaspoon salt
6 tablespoons brandy or whiskey

Method Preheat the oven to 180°C / Gas 4.

First make the pastry. Sieve the flour and icing sugar in a bowl. Add the butter, egg yolk, water and lemon juice. Beat with an electric mixer at slow speed until the mixture forms a dough.

Place the pastry in greaseproof paper or clingfilm and put in the fridge for at least 30 minutes before use. Roll out 2/3 of the pastry thinly on a lightly floured board. Cut out rounds with a cutter a little larger than the tartlet tins. Line the tins with rounds of pastry. Put 1 tablespoon of mincemeat in each.

Roll out the remainder of the pastry and cut with a slightly smaller cutter to fit the tops. Brush the edges of the mince pies with water and place the smaller rounds on top. Seal with the tips of your fingers. Make a small slit in each mince pie. Brush with beaten egg. Bake in the oven for 15-20 minutes. Leave the pies to cool in the tin before lifting out. Dust with icing sugar.

Mincemeat
Mix all ingredients together in a large bowl, cover with a tea towel and leave overnight. Mix well next day and pack into sterilised, spotlessly clean dry jars. Seal and store in a cool dark place for 3-4 weeks before use.

●Tip Why not make twice the amount of mincemeat and put it in some sterililsed fancy jars? Wrap a red ribbon around it and give a jar to your friends for Christmas.

Post-Christmas Turkey Stroganoff

Serves 4

This is a great dish to serve up on St. Stephen's Day, using that lovely leftover turkey, introducing some very non-Christmas flavours and guaranteed to be devoured by all the family. You won't hear anyone moaning that it's 'turkey again'. In fact this is so good, you might want to make it all year round – in that case try using leftover chicken instead.

Ingredients

1 ½lb / 700 g cooked turkey breast, cubed
1 tablespoon olive oil
1 large onion, diced
¼ pint / 150 ml dry white wine
5 scallions, sliced

½ pint / 275 ml double cream
2 teaspoons Dijon mustard
1 rounded tablespoon chopped herbs e.g. parsley, basil and mint
12 oz / 350 g basmati and wild rice
Seasoning

Method Heat the oil in a large heavy-bottomed frying-pan and add the onion. Sweat for 3-4 minutes or until the onions are soft. Pour in the wine and cook until the liquid has reduced by half. Now add the cooked turkey, scallions, cream, and mustard. Cook for 5 more minutes. Season to taste.

Meanwhile, cook the rice according to the packet instructions and drain it. Keep warm until ready to serve.

To Serve Spoon the rice into a bowl and pile on the stroganoff. Sprinkle with the herbs and you're all set to sing along to the rerun of *The Sound of Music*!

● **Tip** This dish can be made with uncooked turkey or chicken. But you must then add the meat with the onions and cook them together for at least 15-20 minutes. Then continue following the recipe.

AL DENTE The texture of properly cooked pasta. Literally 'to the tooth' (Italian), it describes the slight resistance in the pasta when bitten.

BAIN-MARIE Literally 'Mary's bath' (French). When food is cooked in a tray which is placed inside a larger tray half-filled with simmering water. This results in a gentle heat, necessary for delicate dishes like custards.

BAKE BLIND To pre-bake pastry in a tin without a filling, so that it will not later become soggy when cooked with a moist filling. Line the pastry with foil and fill with dried beans, peas or 'baking beans' to prevent puffing up.

BAKING BEANS Special metal or ceramic weights used to fill a lined pastry case when 'baking blind'. Dried beans, peas, lentils etc can be substituted.

BASTE To spoon or brush a liquid (dripping from the pan, butter, fats or a marinade) over foods during roasting or grilling to keep moist.

BLANCH To parboil by immersing in rapidly boiling water for a few seconds or minutes.

CARAMELISE To heat (particularly under a grill) so that the natural sugars in the food burn slightly and go brown. Sugar can also be sprinkled on food to create this effect, as in crème brûlée.

COULIS Fruit that is sweetened with sugar and thinned with water, then puréed to form a fruit sauce or garnish for desserts.

CUSTARD A cooked or baked mixture, mainly of eggs and milk.

DICE To cut into very small cubes of similar size and shape.

DREDGE To coat food with flour or other powdered ingredient.

DRIZZLE To sprinkle drops of liquid erratically over food, usually for garnish.

FOLD To blend two mixtures together gently, releasing as little air as possible. Cut gently through the mixture with a spatula or whisk, from the bottom to the top, rotating the bowl constantly, until thoroughly mixed.

GELATINE An unflavoured substance which gives body to mousses and desserts, and aids setting. Available in leaves or powdered form.

GRATIN ('au gratin'): Any oven-baked dish covered with a golden-brown crust of cheese, breadcrumbs or creamy sauce.

HULL To remove the tough part of fruit under the stalk.

JULIENNE To cut vegetables or fruits into long thin strips.

MARINADE An acidic-based liquid mixture combining various seasonings used to flavour and tenderise (particularly in meat cookery). Brush food with the mixture or marinate by immersing in it and leaving for at least 1-3 hours but preferably overnight.

MARINATE (also 'marinade'): To soak in a marinade.

PIN-BONED To remove fish-bones from a fillet of round fish. Kitchen pliers or tweezers set aside for the purpose can be used.

POACH To cook very gently in any liquid kept just below boiling point.

PURÉE To mash until perfectly smooth, either by hand, by putting through a sieve or by mixing in a blender or food processor.

REDUCE To simmer a liquid until much of the moisture evaporates.

REFRESH To dip into cold water or run cold water over food that has been parboiled or 'blanched' in hot water. This stops food from cooking any further.

ROUX A mixture of butter, margarine or any fat and flour, cooked for 1-2 minutes over a medium heat. Used as a thickening agent.

SAUTÉ To cook gently in a small amount of oil or butter on a low heat. Also used to brown food.

SEAL To brown very quickly on all sides to seal in juices and flavour and improve appearance and colour.

SEASONING A mixture of three parts salt to one part ground pepper.

SIMMER To keep a liquid or sauce at a point just below boiling-point. When simmering, small bubbles will rise slowly to the surface, usually breaking before they reach it.

SWEAT To cook slowly in oil or butter.

SYRUP Sugar dissolved in liquid, usually water, over a medium heat. Syrup cooked until most of the liquid has evaporated becomes a caramel sauce.

WILT To cook until limp e.g. vegetables.

ZEST Thin outer coloured layer of a citrus fruit's skin. Can be removed with a special zester, a vegetable peeler or a grater.